TEXAS HOMES OF THE NINETEENTH CENTURY

PUBLICATION NUMBER ONE

The Texas Architectural Survey

SPONSORED BY THE

AMON CARTER MUSEUM OF WESTERN ART

AND THE

SCHOOL OF ARCHITECTURE, THE UNIVERSITY OF TEXAS

TEXAS HOMES
OF THE
NINETEENTH
CENTURY

Photographs by TODD WEBB

Text by DRURY BLAKELEY ALEXANDER

FOREWORD BY HARRY H. RANSOM

PUBLISHED FOR THE *Amon Carter Museum of Western Art*

BY THE UNIVERSITY OF TEXAS PRESS · AUSTIN & LONDON

Library of Congress Catalog Card No. 66–27416
Copyright © 1966 by Amon Carter Museum of Western Art
Manufactured in the United States of America
by Kingsport Press, Inc., Kingsport, Tennessee

The Amon Carter Museum of Western Art was established under the will of the late Amon G. Carter for the study and documentation of westering North America. The program of the Museum is expressed in publications, exhibitions, and permanent collections related to the many aspects of American culture, both historic and contemporary, which find their identification as Western.

Mitchell A. Wilder, *Director*
Amon Carter Museum of Western Art

FOREWORD

The two decades since World War II have seen greater change than any similar period of history. Possibly the greatest change has been the subtlest one: the development of a vivid awareness of many things—ideas, values, assets, and deficiencies—mixed in a bewildering present which we struggle to understand and a past which we have come at last to cherish. The most visible reminders of another time in the life of the state are architectural. We have lived with old buildings from childhood and have usually taken them for granted. Now we are dismayed by each plan for their obliteration.

If Texas has been negligent of her architectural past, the state shares a common fault. The preservation of buildings, a profound concern of students and antiquarians, has seldom been uppermost in the American conscience. In more recent years, however, increasing attention has been given to the cause of preservation.

The case for the present survey of architecturally important structures in Texas was clearly underlined by Professor Alexander's discovery that more than twenty significant buildings have been lost since the survey started in 1964. A year earlier the officers of the Amon Carter Museum, in Fort Worth, invited the School of Architecture at The University of Texas to assist in establishing criteria and guidelines for a project to record the spaces and structures in which earlier Texans lived and worked. Field operations started in February 1964 and continued through 1965.

The Texas Architecture Survey will never be completed in the literal sense of that term. Many more structures will be located and photographed, data recorded, publications issued. For this reason the University of Texas, through the School of Architecture at Austin, will maintain permanent files for historians and students. As a continuing study of the past, the Survey will enrich understanding of frontier society and bring an earlier Texas alive.

Harry H. Ransom, Chancellor
The University of Texas
Austin

ACKNOWLEDGMENTS

The text of this book was made possible through a research grant from The University of Texas Research Institute and a leave of absence from the School of Architecture for the academic year 1965–1966. The major portion of the material used in developing the text was collected by The Texas Architecture Survey, a joint project of the Amon Carter Museum of Western Art and the School of Architecture of The University of Texas. The survey was carried out by the field director, John C. Garner, Jr., to whom credit is due for his excellent work in discovering hundreds of worthy examples of Texas architecture. Our gratitude and appreciation go to all of those who were so generous with their time and knowledge in helping Mr. Garner in the survey, especially the county judges, members of county historical survey committees, local historians, librarians, and interested citizens. Nancy Reeves McAdams, librarian for the School of Architecture, The University of Texas, who compiled a bibliography of Texas Architecture, has been most helpful. Special appreciation and thanks go to Marian B. Davis, professor of art, Robert B. Rettig, visiting assistant professor of architecture, and Natalie Noble Morgan for reading the typescript and making many helpful suggestions for its improvement. The drawings in the text were done by Michael D. Utsey, a fifth-year student in the School of Architecture.

Drury B. Alexander
Austin, Texas

CONTENTS

TEXAS ARCHITECTURE AS VISUAL HISTORY

HISTORIES of Texas usually begin with the earliest Spanish explorations of the Gulf of Mexico, some four hundred years ago. The Texas we know, however, is just under a century and a half old, for it came into being in the nineteenth century. During the brief period from 1820 to 1880 Texas changed from a wilderness to an agricultural state, from a vaguely defined subdivision of a Spanish colony to one of the United States. In the process it became first a state of Mexico, then an independent republic, and for a brief time one of the Confederate States of America. From a land sparsely inhabited by Indian tribes, a few Spanish missionaries, and soldiers, it developed into a state whose population, of over three million in 1900, was predominantly Anglo-American. The advent of colonists and settlers from the United States, who were eventually to take over the state, began in the 1820's. By 1845, after the passage of a quarter of a century, the colorful history of the birth of Texas had been written; prominent in the legend were names of such people as Austin, Crockett, Bowie, Travis, and Houston, of such places and events as the Alamo, Goliad, and San Jacinto.

The purpose of this book is to capture in photographs the amazing variety and richness of the architectural heritage left to us by these first settlers and those who came after them. Unlike the heritage of the eastern states, with their colonial and Georgian examples from the seventeenth and eighteenth centuries, that of Texas is of the nineteenth century, and in the architecture of this period we find reflected the forces and events which give the state its special character. The rich variety of this nineteenth-century architecture can still be seen in Texas: in the quiet streets of the "Southern" towns of East Texas, in the courthouse squares of the county seats in Central Texas, in the few remaining monuments of Victorian grandeur in the larger cities, in the houses of the German colonists of Central Texas, where are revealed national traditions from Europe, and in the border towns of Spanish-Mexican character. In these and many more types the history of Texas is seen. Every year this store of visual history is eroded by man and nature; here, preserved on these pages, is a sample of what is left today. Tomorrow, we can be sure, will possess even less.

This nineteenth-century Texas architecture is for the most part anonymous architecture, that is, architecture built by unknown builders. Few men in Texas were trained in the profession of architecture before 1900, and these were mainly the men responsible for the larger Victorian houses and public buildings. The character of Texas homes before 1900 is the result of the strong influence of the cultural origins of the builders—in most cases also the owners. As a result, the houses of this period reflect clearly the background, aims, and ambitions of the builders, as well as the limitations of the frontier environment. While creating a new state the early Texans were also creating new homes, and in studying their homes we shall learn much about them, their cultural background, their training, and their everyday life.

Just as architecture reflects the time and place of its origin, so a knowledge of Texas history provides an insight into Texas architecture. A brief summary of the major historical developments in Texas will help us to understand why certain characteristics appear in Texas houses and why others are absent. This approach will confirm our assumptions concerning such things as the national origin of the builder who uses a particular type of wood joint or a special way of handling masonry. It will add to our enjoyment of these houses just as the houses add to our understanding of Texas history.

The first of the six flags to fly over the territory of Texas was planted by Spain in the sixteenth century when Álvarez de Piñeda mapped the Gulf Coast from Florida to Vera Cruz in 1519. After a period of neglect by the Spanish, La Salle, in 1685, raised the French flag of Louis XIV over Fort St. Louis. This action brought the attention of Spain back to Texas, and in the eighteenth century Spanish activity in Texas reached its highest level with the establishment of a chain of missions stretching from the Rio Grande across central Texas and as far east as Louisiana.

It was during the period of Spanish missionary activity that the first significant examples of Western European architecture were built in Texas. This architecture consisted primarily of missions, forts, and magisterial headquarters. For, instead of colonists, Spain sent missionaries and soldiers into Texas, and, because of this failure to colonize, her control was short-lived. Spain's architectural influence in this early period, therefore, is seen only in the fine mission churches, which are charming provincial examples of the late Spanish Renaissance or Baroque style as it was imported from Spain by way of Mexico. Of the few sectarian houses built by the Spanish of this period little remains except the Governor's Palace in San Antonio, which was in reality the Comandancia built in 1749.[1]

Spanish influence, however, reappeared in the nineteenth century in the houses of San Antonio and in the border towns of Brownsville, Rio Grande City, and Roma.

[1] Ernest Allen Connally, "Texas Architecture," *Historic Preservation,* Vol. 16, No. 6 (November–December, 1964), p. 222.

As a result, a few houses using Spanish *palisado* construction (walls which are built of vertical posts or poles placed side by side and either stuck in the ground or set on a log beam) may yet be found in San Antonio, and brick or adobe houses of Spanish and Mexican origin are typical of the Rio Grande Valley towns.

Because Texas was settled in the nineteenth century it was then that the pattern of its development, the growth of its cities, and the character of its regions took form. At the beginning of the century there were only three established settlements—San Antonio, Goliad, and Nacogdoches. Although American families had been pushing into Texas since the beginning of the century, organized colonization by Americans was not accomplished until 1821. At this time Stephen F. Austin sponsored a colony of three hundred settlers, thus carrying out the plans of his father, Moses Austin, who died before realizing his dream of colonizing Texas. The permission to bring in three hundred families was given by the Spanish government, and the first settlements in the Austin colony were made late in 1821, at Columbus, on the Colorado, and at Washington-on-the-Brazos. In spite of problems arising from the unsettled conditions in Mexico which culminated in Mexico's independence from Spain, and the necessity for renegotiation of the colonization grant, Austin's colony grew and was followed by a number of other colonies. In July, 1823, Austin's colonists established as the headquarters of the colony San Felipe de Austin, which became the unofficial capital of all of the Anglo-American settlements. As a result of the influx of families from the United States the Anglo-American element of the population became dominant, and in a period of fifteen years the number of settlers grew from 7,000 to between 35,000 and 50,000.

These settlers, referred to as "Anglo-Americans," were primarily the descendants of the English and Scots who, several generations earlier, had settled along the Atlantic coast. Later they had moved westward into Tennessee, Kentucky, Alabama, Georgia, and Mississippi. The men who came to Texas, many of them younger sons, were looking for land they could call their own and were continuing a tradition which had by now become a way of life in this new, frontier-oriented land. Always seeking fertile farming country, they quickly laid claim to the richest land available in Texas—the coastal plains, the black-land prairies, and the rich East Texas woodlands. Among these pioneer adventurers were men such as Gail Borden and his brothers.

It was only natural that the ties and sympathies of these colonists were with their kinsmen in the United States. This, together with the fact that Mexico was torn by political unrest and instability and was in their minds a "foreign" land, made any successful relationship between the Mexican government and the Texas colonists extremely difficult. It is generally acknowledged that the majority of the Anglo-American colonists came into Texas in good faith and with the intention of remaining citizens of the Republic of Mexico. It also seems likely that the Texans would not have revolted if Santa Anna or the Mexican government had carried out their responsibilities to the colonists fairly and impartially. A series of unpopular laws, passed in 1830, increased the dissatisfaction of the colonists. These laws infringed upon certain rights which the Anglo-American Texans considered fundamental—for example, trial by jury.

In 1835, after several unsuccessful attempts to gain concessions from the Mexican government, Austin returned to Texas from Mexico convinced that a war for independence was inevitable. Following a series of incidents which intensified the growing distrust on both sides, President Santa Anna established a military force to rule over Texas-Coahuila. On October 2, 1835, a Mexican company, sent to Gonzales to take possession of a cannon, was attacked and defeated by the Texans. This, the Battle of Gonzales, marked the beginning of the Texas Revolution. On April 21, 1836, after a series of fateful events including the fall of the Alamo and the Goliad Massacre, the Texans, under General Sam Houston, won their independence at the Battle of San Jacinto.

In the first election following the establishment of the Republic of Texas, Sam Houston was elected president. During the period of the Republic, 1836–1845 colonization was encouraged and many new settlements were made. The site of the capital of the Republic was selected in 1839, and the name Austin was given to the new seat of government. By 1845 the population of Texas had increased to something between 125,000 and 150,000.

Although the major increase in population was due to immigration from the United States, during this period also a number of significant European colonies were established in Texas. The architecture of the first half of the nineteenth century is characterized first by the frontier house types brought into Texas by the Anglo-American settlers—the log house and the frame house—and secondly by the European house types introduced by the large number of colonists who came into Texas from Germany, Alsace, France, and Switzerland, and by the Spanish and Mexican influences along the border and in San Antonio. Of the various European colonists who came into Texas at this time, the Germans were by far the largest in numbers. Due to unsettled economic, religious, and political conditions in Germany, many enterprising and idealistic German families sought the freedom and opportunity of a new land. By 1847 more than 7,000 Germans had settled in Texas. Brought over under the patronage of a group of noblemen who organized a society to promote a German colony in the free Republic of Texas, these industrious citizens brought with them a rich cultural heritage which is still evident in the areas of Central Texas where they settled. The homes which they built are a fascinating reminder of the medieval building techniques of Europe, for these were the techniques which they carried with them into the wilderness of nineteenth-century Texas.

The house types found in Texas in the first half of the nineteenth century are the double log house and the frame house of the Anglo-American settlers, the adobe and *palisado* houses of the Mexicans, and the medieval half-timber or *Fachwerk* houses of the German colonists. In addition, masonry houses were built by all three groups where wood was scarce and stone could be easily worked. Many of the homes of these three cultural groups still survive to give us an idea of the life of these early Texans, or "Texians," as those who settled before the annexation styled themselves.

On December 29, 1845, Texas became the twenty-eighth state of the United States of America. The period of early statehood, from 1845 to 1861, the year when Texas seceded from the Union and joined the Confederacy, was one of rapid development and prosperity. The cities of East and Central Texas became more and more Southern in their cultural pattern, and from simple frontier settlements they evolved into smaller versions of such Southern cities as Memphis, Atlanta, and Natchez. One of the most obvious characteristics of the frontier is the style lag. New modes in architecture, in dress, and in the arts of living were first introduced in the major cities on the Atlantic coast, where they were usually imported from England. The pioneer, pushing the frontiers westward, had neither the time nor the money to keep up; as a result, the style of his house, his furniture, and his clothing was not of the latest fashion. The Greek Revival, first seen in the East in the 1820's, reached Texas in the 1840's. From 1840 until 1870 it was the accepted style for residential architecture in Texas, retaining its popularity for a period of five years or so after the Civil War, which had generally marked the end of its favor in the rest of the country. The reluctance to discard it for the more flamboyant Victorian is an indication of the late arrival of the industrial age in Texas.

The transition from the East Texas house, the pioneer log house, and the German house to the Classic Revival or Greek Revival style of the '40's and '50's was an easy and logical one. Some characteristic features of the Greek Revival—the symmetrical alignment of windows on either side of the entrance, the columnar porch or gallery, and the symmetrical arrangement of rooms on either side of a central hall—were already parts of the building pattern of Texans, both Anglo-American and German. The Mexican buildings, still Renaissance in character, thus had retained their formal, symmetrical balance and their basic classicism in detail. The change to Greek Revival was primarily a change in scale, proportion, and detail. The houses were generally larger, and the proportional emphasis was one of classic horizontality rather than medieval verticality; the detail was as correctly classic as the builders' skill, resources, and knowledge could provide.

As in all parts of the United States, and particularly in the South, so in Texas the Greek Revival style provided some of the finest residential architecture. Although the rigid formality of plan proved to be its downfall in the end, the adaptability and the simplicity of its detail made it one of the most successful styles in the history of American architecture. From the grandest Natchez mansion to the simplest cottage, from the most elegant Corinthian column to the plainest capped post, the serenity and grace of the style were easily achieved. With the introduction of this style it was clear that civilization had caught up with the frontier. If one considers the problems of establishing settlements in a new land and the state of communications between the Eastern states and the inland prairies, twenty years was not so long a time.

The Greek Revival style has become almost the symbol of the Old South, even to the point of being popularly referred to as "Southern Colonial." It is true that as a style it was ideally suited to the climate and the culture of the South of that romantic era which was terminated by the Civil War. The term is a misnomer, however, for as a style it was neither Southern nor colonial, since it first appeared in Philadelphia and other Northern cities, becoming popular throughout the East and North as well as the South, and since it dates from 1820, some three decades after the American Revolution.

Change is the inevitable result of war, and the society which was so flatteringly reflected in the Greek Revival was destroyed by that tragic event, the Civil War. Following the War came the Reconstruction Period, which ended in Texas in 1873. By this time the state was already showing signs of the rapid development and prosperity which marked the last quarter of the nineteenth century in Texas. The western half of the state was settled during this post-Civil War period, and cattle soon ranked with cotton and lumber as one of the principal sources of wealth. Until the Civil War, river boats and ox-drawn wagon trains were the means of supplying the interior with both necessities and luxuries. Now the railroads came in, and soon the state was criss-crossed by a network of lines, which provided facilities for shipping more cotton, lumber, and cattle to the markets, with the resultant increase in wealth in Texas. The dramatic change which the railroads brought about in communication cannot be overemphasized. Neither the automobile nor the airplane, significant as they are, has had a more revolutionary effect on the lives of the people and the development of the state than did the railroads. When their appearance obliterated the frontier, the style lag which is characteristic of the frontier disappeared. When travel and shipping were done by water, the major cultural influences came in from New Orleans and other southern ports to Galveston, Jefferson, and Brazoria. Now the railroads linked Texas directly with the eastern centers. The citizens of Houston, Galveston, San Antonio, and Austin could buy the same furniture and clothing, could employ the same architectural styles, as those current in New York, Memphis, St. Louis, and New Orleans. The cattlemen went to markets in Kansas City, St. Louis, or Chicago; the cotton planters went to Memphis, New Orleans, and Atlanta. Cast-iron ornament made in Philadelphia dressed up the galleries of Victorian mansions in Galveston, San Antonio, and Austin; and Belter furniture and Brussels lace curtains filled their parlors.

The exuberant Victorian style coincided with the newly established society and fittingly expressed it. Lining the oak-shaded main streets of East Texas towns were the big gabled and turreted mansions "built by cotton." In Fort Worth, San Antonio, and Gonzales they would be "built by cattle," and in Beaumont and Orange, "built by lumber." By far the most fascinating architecture in Texas is that of the last two decades of the nineteenth century. It was during this period that architecture was the primary means of expressing wealth, pride, ambition, and self-satisfaction. The era of great courthouses, churches, railroad stations, and homes was at hand.

In fewer than one hundred years Texas had emerged from a wilderness to a civilized state. The frontier, moving westward, had passed through, to be replaced by an established, well organized, soundly based society.

When we examine the houses of nineteenth-century Texas, we find that they fall into three major stylistic groups which correspond generally to the historic periods in the settlement and growth of the state. The first period will be called frontier-settlement architecture; the second, ante-bellum South; and the third, the American Victorian.

FRONTIER-SETTLEMENT ARCHITECTURE

ALTHOUGH the Spanish and Mexican population in Texas had built a few houses prior to 1800, these were extremely primitive adobe or *palisado* structures. The log houses of the Anglo-American settlers represent the first house type with architectural significance in the state.

The log house and the log cabin were the ideal solutions for the frontiersman, at least as long as the frontier was in wooded territory. A simple distinction defines the difference between these two types of log structure: the log house is constructed of square hewn logs; the cabin is built of round logs. Certainly, the history of the log house is a part of the history of the westward expansion of the United States. Just when the log cabin was first used in the North American colonies is not certain. Some maintain that it was introduced into this country by the Swedes who settled along the Delaware River in 1638. Others believe that such a logical method of building would have been developed by any settlers in a country where trees are plentiful and tools are scarce. Whatever its origin, it soon became the standard house type of the pioneer. This form was associated particularly with the Scotch-Irish as they settled North Carolina and Tennessee and with the English who moved westward from Virginia over the Blue Ridge Mountains into Kentucky. The simplicity of the log cabin and its ease of construction, requiring little more than an axe and the labor of one family, made it the obvious choice of the pioneer. This, together with the abundance of logs which resulted from clearing the land for farming, gave the log cabin pre-eminence as a frontier structure.

Anglo-Americans, from the beginning of their settlement in Texas, seem to have built two types of log structure, the one usually referred to as the log cabin, which used round logs, and the log house, with its square hewn logs. The round logs of the log cabin were notched with a saddlelike cut on top and bottom some distance from the end of the log, a method which required that the logs project, sometimes as much as a foot, beyond the joints of each corner. This type of joint (Fig. 1) was the most characteristic feature of the log cabin. The log house, however, is a type of construction requiring more time and greater skill with the axe, perhaps also with a saw. For this type of house the logs were hewn so as to be flat on all four sides and the joints were carefully cut to fit in either a rabbeted (Fig. 2) or a dovetail (Fig. 3) joint with no extension of the logs at the corners.

The usual practice for the pioneer family was to build a log cabin as soon as they had settled on their land, this being the fastest-erected type of structure that would afford adequate protection from the elements, the animals, and the Indians. Then, as the settler had time, he would begin his log house, which, with its hewn logs and fitted joints, would take considerably more time. As a home the log house was much superior to the cabin, its hewn logs

1. *Saddle-Notched Log Joint*

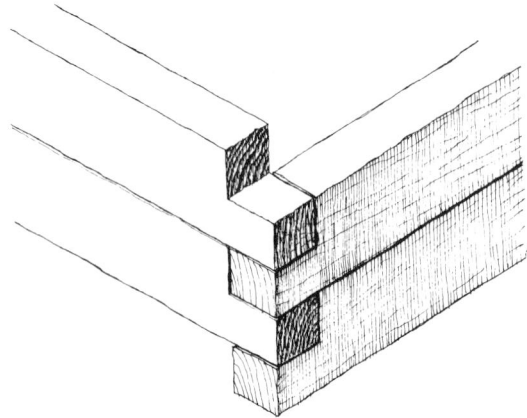

2. *Rabbeted Hewn-Log Joint*

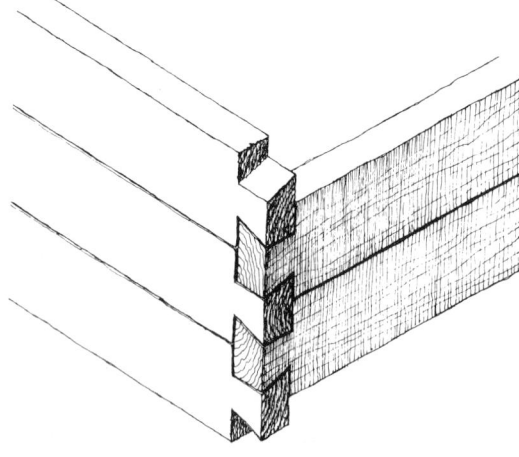

3. *Dovetail Hewn-Log Joint*

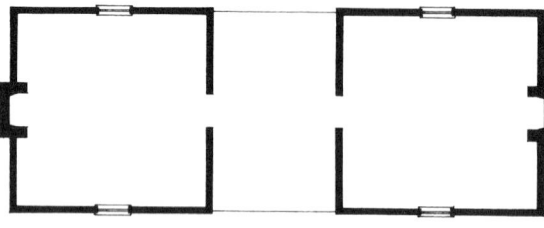

4. *Two-Room, or Dog-Run, Plan*

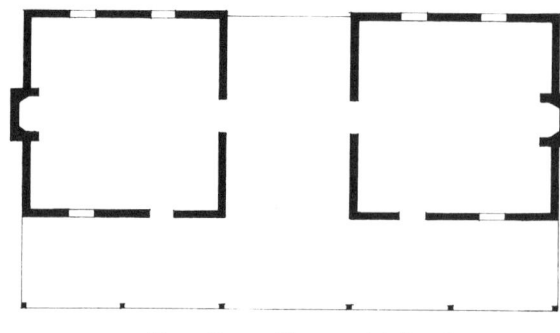

5. *Two-Room House with Porch*

being so tightly fitted that chinking between the logs was virtually unnecessary. Being more weatherproof, it was more comfortable and much more permanent. Many old examples of log houses can still be found, but very few truly old log cabins are still standing. The saddle-notched joints of the log cabin held water, thus inducing rot, while the dovetail joints (Fig. 3) of the log houses were cut so that all surfaces sloped outward to drain the water off, thus preserving the wood.

The roofs of both the log cabin and the log house were simple gable roofs with the ridges parallel to the front of the houses. The plan provided either one or two rooms, with the attic space frequently utilized for sleeping. If the house was a single room it would have one door opening to the front, a chimney at one end, and usually one small window on each of the remaining two sides. These windows were closed by solid shutters made in the same way as the door. There might be also one or two small slit openings in the fireplace wall to be used as rifle ports in case of an Indian attack. If the house consisted of two rooms, it would most likely have an open hall—sometimes called a "dog run" or "dog trot"—between the two rooms, providing a pleasant place for summer living and an area for hanging the wash on rainy days and for storing meat and other foodstuffs in winter (Fig. 4). In the two-room-and-hall type of house the doors would open onto the hall; if a porch extended across the front the doors might also open onto it (Fig. 5). This was the house type that was brought across the Appalachians into Kentucky and Tennessee, and this was the house type that the pioneer brought into Texas.

Although both the frontiersman and the planter would probably build a log cabin for immediate shelter, these houses were not looked upon as permanent homes, and few if any of the original log cabins remain from the earliest Anglo-American settlements. The planter would soon build himself a frame house with some resemblance to the kind he had known in Virginia, the Carolinas, Georgia, or the nearer Southern states, while the frontiersman would build a log house, since he would have to build his house without the help of slaves.

The early log houses were often covered at a later date with siding or weatherboarding. Upon close inspection many old East Texas farmhouses which appear to be frame and weatherboard houses turn out to be log houses dressed up with the typical lapped siding or clapboard of a later period. Log cabins and log houses were to be found throughout the Anglo-American settlements in Texas, from the Red River to the Gulf Coast and from the Sabine to the Colorado.

During this time, in addition to log houses, the more sophisticated houses of timber frame were being constructed. Unlike the modern frame house built of light two-by-fours, made possible by the steam-powered sawmills, the early Texas frame house was a heavy skeleton cage of square hewn logs with diagonal timbers notched and pegged to the corner uprights, a building method in

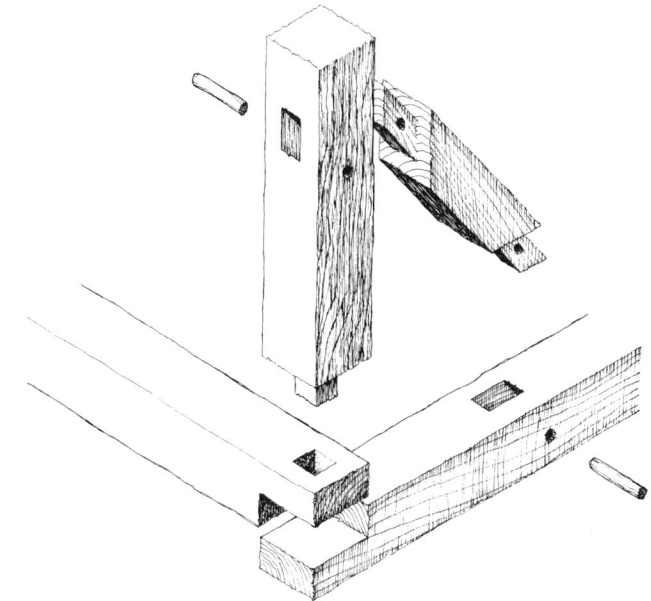

6. *Detail of Braced-Frame Construction*

use from medieval times and brought to this country by the English settlers in the seventeenth century (Fig. 6). A later group of immigrants, the German settlers, brought to Texas their own version of this medieval construction. The frame house requires more skill to construct than the log house, its joints being of the mortise-and-tenon, or rabbet, type, but it requires less material, since it is a frame wall rather than a solid, log-upon-log wall. The frame house, of course, always requires some type of exterior sheathing, generally weatherboarding. Occasionally the interior might be left with the exposed frame, but usually it was sheathed with flush or smooth board walls, as was the ceiling. The joints between the boards on the ceiling, and sometimes on the walls, were frequently covered with narrow battens or strips of wood.

The plan of the frame house was essentially the same as that of the log house. Each had two possibilities—one room or two rooms. The one-room house had a chimney on one side and a door more or less centered on the front. A few houses, of course, had more than two rooms, but the basic arrangement was not changed. The ridge of the gable roof would be parallel to the front of the house. Windows in the earlier examples were scarce and small and closed with battened shutters. The two-room house would usually have an open hall or dog run between and a porch across the front, especially with the frame house. This type of frame house, which is typical of those built in the upper and middle south—Tennessee, Kentucky, Alabama, Georgia, Mississippi, and Arkansas—was the basic Texas House and has become specialized in its form in East Texas to the extent that it is recognized there as the East Texas House.[1] The examples we have chosen for presentation are scattered across East and South Central Texas and reveal the general spread of this type of structure from the very earliest Anglo-American settlements down to the end of the nineteenth century, when this type of frame house was still the predominant form for the small Texas farmhouse. So common did this frame house become during the greater part of the nineteenth century, the period of development in Texas, that it deserves the title Early Texas House.

Our knowledge of the homes of the earliest settlers in Texas comes from those houses which are still standing and from the accounts of early travellers through Texas who have left us their impressions of the homes of the pioneer settlers. The account of Frederick Olmsted in *A Journey through Texas, 1857*, is perhaps the best known.

A more graphic presentation is to be found in the sketchbook of Captain Seth Eastman, U.S. Army, who was assigned to Texas in 1848. His sketches, depicting his journey down the Mississippi from Sainte Genevieve to the Gulf and from Indian Point (Indianola), Texas, into central Texas, are both informative and delightful. These sketches give us a contemporary picture of the Mississippi River and of Texas in the 1840's, as well as a fascinating pictorial review of the movement of the pioneer cabin and frame house from the South into Texas. The record begins with a sketch of a log house eight miles above Sainte Genevieve; it continues with a one-room cabin in a clearing by Devil's Bake Oven; and then follow another crude log cabin or crib and a very good example of the frame, weatherboarded house in Arkansas below Helena. Then he shows, above New Orleans, the typical Louisiana plantation houses, with wide gambrel roofs overhanging the enclosing galleries.

After a boat trip from Louisiana, Captain Eastman landed at Indianola. In his Texas sketches we see landscapes known to us today; especially familiar are his sketches of post and live oaks. At Seguin he pictures a town of log houses and then gives a fine drawing of one double log house showing the rail-fenced yard and the open hall or dog run. After a few sketches of missions and houses in San Antonio, the Captain moves on to Fredericksburg, where he was obviously captivated by the "Dutch" houses. From these pages we have a marvelous picture of Fredericksburg in 1849, from log cabins to medieval *Fachwerk,* the traditional half-timber construction which marks the German colonial architecture in Texas.

[1] Elliot A. P. Evans, "The East Texas House," *SAHJ,* Vol. 11, No. 4 (December, 1952), pp. 1–7.

Another account by an early traveller to Texas is that of Mary Austin Holley, a cousin of Stephen F. Austin and one of the most interesting women in early Texas history. Perhaps the most fascinating item among the numerous books and articles which she wrote on Texas is a small diary that she kept while on one of her trips to Texas. This diary, including miniature sketches of houses and scenes along her journey, gives a candid picture of the conditions in the new colony and the life of the Anglo-American settlers there.

The description of Texas by the German geologist, Ferdinand Roemer, who travelled over the state during 1845–1847, presents, as we might expect, the acute observations of a man who was trained to observe and whose intentions were to relate his findings to his fellow countrymen. His description of the manor house of the plantation Nassau, owned by Count von Boos-Waldeck, a leader in the organization of German noblemen which was founded to colonize Germans in Texas, is especially informative:

The whole house is built of rough hewn oak logs carefully grooved, lying horizontally over each other. It is separated into two parts, according to the custom of the country, forming in the center an open, covered passage, which offers the inhabitants a cool, pleasant resort in summer. The two longer sides of the house face north and south so that the prevailing south winds in summer can circulate freely through the hall. On these two sides, the roof projects about ten feet and is supported by wooden pillars forming the aforementioned galleries, whose floors are two feet above the ground. On each end of the house is a fireplace built of ashlar stones reaching several feet above the top of the house which gives to the whole building a stately appearance. Most of the farm houses of Texas have fireplaces built of thin logs which are placed over each other to form a square. The cracks are filled with mud or clay.

Next to the manor house stands an ordinary log house occupied by a negro family, the servants of the household. The head of this family was a very valuable negro, who among other accomplishments thoroughly understood the trade of blacksmith and who could easily have earned three dollars a day at this trade. Several times he could have been sold for two thousand dollars. Since he always conducted himself properly, he was treated with a certain consideration and he boasted that during thirty years he had not received a single beating from his master. A German overseer of the plantation, inexperienced in the handling of negroes, decided to whip him on account of a supposed disobedience, just as was done to the ordinary negro working in the field, but he opposed this and ran away, and could only be induced to return on the assurance that he would not be punished. Nor need one wonder that the consciousness of human dignity awakens in such negroes who in accomplishments and cultural advancement are almost equal to the whites.

. . . The farm buildings belonging to the plantation lie about a gunshot distant from the manor house at the foot of the hill. There are barns, storage houses, negro cabins and a house for the overseer. All are rough log houses made of roughly hewn logs, covered with shingles, which, like most buildings of this kind on an American plantation have no particular pleasing appearance, and in neatness and substantial construction do not compare with the farm building of a large German estate.[2]

The largest number of German colonial houses, of course, are to be found in Fredericksburg. Seeking to escape the economic and political difficulties in Germany during the eighteen-thirties and forties, these colonists transplanted a considerable measure of their native German culture in central Texas, and today the homes which they built bear witness to their German heritage. Like the

[2] Ferdinand Roemer, *Texas,* p. 163.

Anglo-American colonists, the Germans first built log cabins; then, as soon as they could manage, they built more suitable homes, houses like those they had known in their mother country. These houses, however, were modified by the influences of the new environment. The climate, the materials available, the frontier life, and the Indians, all had their effect on the modification of the traditional German house which these colonists were attempting to build in their new homeland.

The first of the characteristics which mark the German colonial architecture is the proportion. The German colonial house, usually two rooms deep, tended to be nearly square in plan, in contrast to the Anglo-American house, which was usually one room deep, emphasizing breadth rather than depth. The resulting roof lines were therefore different and easily distinguishable. Roof slopes, proportions, and outlines are like speech accents in that they are among the first things that give away the nationality of the builder. Like speech accents, however, they are subtle, and experience is required to distinguish them. The square, blocklike form of the German house is surmounted by a high gable roof which rises sometimes as high again as the walls of the house, and whose angle is usually greater than that of the Anglo-American house. Because of the climate the German colonists quickly adopted the porch or gallery, a feature of the Anglo-American house which they had observed as they passed through Galveston, Houston, or San Antonio. This porch across the front of the house usually had a very low-pitched roof which joined the house roof at the eave line or was attached to the front wall of the house below the eave of the main roof.

An interesting variation of the town house, seen in Fredericksburg and in the surrounding countryside, is the Sunday house. These small story-and-a-half cottages were built by farmers who brought their families to town on Saturday for shopping and visiting, remaining overnight in order to attend church on Sunday before returning to their farms. These houses are all very similar, having usually a small porch across the front, and a steeply pitched gable roof with the ridge parallel to the street and with the rear slope broken out to cover a shedlike portion at the rear, the whole structure resembling somewhat the New England salt box house type. An outside stair on one side leads up to a door opening into the gable of the attic, where sleeping space was provided for the boys of the family, who could thereby come in late Saturday night without disturbing the rest of the family.

In their structural techniques the German colonists were more traditional than the Anglo-Americans, and in both their frame and their masonry houses in central Texas, one can recognize the hand of the German craftsman. The frame houses followed the medieval *Fachwerk* method of construction, that is a frame of heavy timbers with diagonal bracing members at the corners and at doors and other openings. This type of braced framing belongs to the very earliest wood-building traditions of Europe. After the frame was built, the spaces between the timbers of the frame were filled in with stone, or wattle and daub (mud plastered on a lattice of twigs), or sun-dried mud bricks. These walls were frequently given a coating of lime plaster, which through the years has been renewed so often that in many cases the frame is no longer visible, and it is difficult to determine whether the house is actually of *Fachwerk*. The details also tell of the German origin of the builder. Casement windows, usually smaller than the Anglo-American windows, arched openings in masonry buildings, and details of wood construction and trim reveal the German tradition. Excellent examples of German houses, in addition to those in Fredericksburg, remain in New Braunfels, La Grange, Round Top, and a number of other small Central Texas towns.

Another center of considerable architectural interest is Castroville, colonized by Henri Castro in 1844 with settlers brought from Alsace, Switzerland, and Germany. This town and nearby Quihi, also settled by Castro, still retain many charming examples of Alsatian house types. These are seen in several houses around the town square of Castroville, which is dominated by the spire of the Neo-Gothic church. Differing somewhat from the Fredericksburg German, these houses reveal more Alsatian characteristics, such as a lower pitch in roof lines, fewer porches, doors (often French doors) and windows opening onto the yard or sidewalk. Two other interesting details to be seen here in the masonry houses are a chimney rising from the peak of the gable at each end of the house and, directly below the chimney, a window, sometimes one in both the ground floor and the attic. This means that the flue, in order to miss the window, must be carried up in the masonry at a very decided slant from a fireplace in the corner of the room. One of the more notable houses in Castroville is the Carle House, a two-story shop-and-dwelling combination facing the square. It is distinguished by a second-floor balcony, or gallery, cantilevered over the sidewalk, which gives it a noticeable south European character. In Castroville and Quihi the houses are mostly of stone, often covered with stucco, the combination giving, in general, a quality different from that of the German colonial houses found in the counties to the north which were settled by immigrants who came from central Germany and whose building traditions were somewhat different from those of the Alsatians.

Numerous other colonial immigrants attempted settlements in Texas, but few architectural traces of their efforts remain. One town which has not been entirely lost is Panna Maria, a Polish settlement established in 1854 in Karnes County. Still standing in this community are a number of good stone houses and a church. Another such community is Norway Mills, where a number of Norwegian families built a community and a mill in the late 1800's.

The Spanish and Mexican influence in Texas is centered in San Antonio and in the border towns along the Rio Grande. The Spanish character of much of old San Antonio, with the exception of the missions, is primarily of the nineteenth century. Descriptions of the city by travellers about the turn of the century tell of a very primitive, simple life with humble dwellings of adobe and jackal, or *palisado* (walls formed by palings placed side by side into the ground and then plastered over with clay or mud). Houses were right on the street with sometimes a court or garden at the back. Their roofs of mud and clay, laid over saplings which were supported by cottonwood or cedar logs, were usually hidden by parapets. Later in the century Spanish or Mediterranean house types appeared in this area, brought in by Mexican families moving into Texas. These houses were generally of brick or stone with low-pitched or flat roofs; they opened directly onto the sidewalk and frequently had a walled garden or court at the back. They often combined the functions of business and residence, with a store on the first floor and the family living quarters on the second. The facades might have classic pilasters and cornices done in molded brick of an extremely high quality, as in the Guerra Building in Roma. Distinctly Spanish in origin, these houses retain the characteristics of the Spanish Renaissance town house, characteristics that were introduced into Mexico in the eighteenth century.

French influence in nineteenth-century Texas was brought primarily from Louisiana by the planters who came from that state and built their houses in the Louisiana tradition. These houses were frequently of the raised-cottage type, with a basement or ground floor completely above the ground and the main floor at the second level, and with a flight of stairs leading from the ground up to the gallery. Their hipped roofs usually have a break in the slope, which produces a graceful sweep as they extend out over the galleries ordinarily encircling the house. The Noble House in Houston is representative of this type. The French Legation in Austin, another fine example of the style, is perhaps the most characteristically French house in Texas, although not raised above ground level. Dormers like those of the French Legation are also a feature of French houses and appear in French architecture much earlier than in the other national styles. Since this style was introduced from Louisiana, it is not a pure French architecture, but, like its Louisiana prototypes, is a blend of French, Spanish, and West Indian elements. Double doors, floor-length casement windows, and hipped roofs with dormers reflect the French tradition, whereas the wide overhanging roof and encircling galleries and the practice of raising the main floor high above the ground to avoid the dampness are due to the tropical climate of the West Indies.

1. *The Jordan Log House, near Huntsville*

2. *The Jordon Log House* (*Detail of Dovetail Joint*), *near Huntsville*

3. *The W. W. Craig House, New Prospect Community*

4. *The Claiborne Kyle Log House, Kyle*

5. *A Rail Fence on Behrens Farm, near Bluffton*

6. *The Warren Log House (Detail of Rabbeted Joint), near Evergreen Community*

7. *The Dabney Log House, near Evergreen Community*

8. *The Montgomery Log House, near Cherokee*

9. *The Dick West Log House, Salem Community*

10. *The Holcomb Log Cabin, near Moscow*

11. *The Eggleston Log House, Gonzales*

12. *The Milton Garrett House, San Augustine*

13. *The W. H. Ledbetter House, Albany*

14. *Barn on Walter Grenwell Farm, Llano County*

15. *The Turner-White-Magee House, Roganville*

16. *The Thomas Barnett House, near Rosenberg*

17. *San Felipe Cottage, Houston*

18. *The Randolph C. Doom House, Bevilport Community*

19. *The Sam Houston House (The Wigwam), Huntsville*

20. *The Sam Houston House (The Wigwam—Hall), Huntsville*

21. *The Captain W. E. Heard House, Egypt*

22. *The W. T. Scott House, Scottsville*

23. *The Jim Odom House, Cherokee Community*

24. *The A. Goldman House, Victoria*

25. *The J. C. Hill House, Maynard Community*

26. *The Sage House, near Starrville*

27. *The Meredith-Hart House, Rio Vista*

28. *The Joseph H. Polley House, La Vernia*

29. *The Captain Nelson Merrell House, Round Rock*

30. *The Humphrey House, Seguin*

31. *The James B. Johnson House, Chireno*

32. *An Old Stage-Coach Station, Independence*

33. *The Tenant House on the Durham Farm, near Hamilton*

34. *A Stone Barn on Austin Street, Mason*

35. *The Stone Water Tower at the J. W. White House, Mason*

36. *The Kammlach House, Fredericksburg*

37. *The Johaan Peter Tatsch House, Fredericksburg*

38. *A House at Bowie and Austin Streets, Fredericksburg*

39. *A Sunday House, Fredericksburg*

40. *The Peter Walter House* (*St. Barnabas Chapel*)*, Fredericksburg*

41. *A Door Detail, Fredericksburg*

42. *The Adrian Edward Conn House, Blanco*

43. *The Adam Schmidt House, near Llano*

44. *The Faltin House, Comfort*

45. *The Judge Stiehl House, La Grange*

46. *The Kreische House, La Grange*

47. *The Stage Coach Inn, Winedale*

48. *The Stage Coach Inn (Ceiling Detail), Winedale*

49. *The Stage Coach Inn (Mantel Detail), Winedale*

50. *Lange's Mill, Doss*

51. *The Peter Lang House, near Castell*

52. *The Dietrich Rode House, Cherry Spring*

53. *The Dietrich Rode House (Barn), Cherry Spring*

54. *The Marschall House, near Prairie Mountain*

55. *A Stone Barn at the Marschall House, near Prairie Mountain*

56. *The Vance House (Landmark Inn), Castroville*

57. *The Vance House (Landmark Inn—Kitchen), Castroville*

58. *The Carle House, Castroville*

59. *A House in Old D'Hanis, Old D'Hanis*

60. *A House in Old D'Hanis, Old D'Hanis*

61. *A House and Barn in Old D'Hanis, Old D'Hanis*

62. *A Palisado House, Bracketville*

63. *Norway Mills, Clifton*

64. *The Noah Cox House, Roma*

ANTE-BELLUM SOUTH ARCHITECTURE

THE EARLY TEXAS house, which was a simple frame structure with a porch across the front, gradually gave way to the more consciously classic forms of the Greek Revival. And yet throughout the nineteenth century, particularly in East Texas, farm houses which retained the characteristics of the Early Texas house were being built. As a result, it is difficult to draw a line between the Early Texas house and the Greek Revival house. Adaptability and ease of simplification were the great advantages of the Greek Revival style. It brought a harmony and dignity to the simplest farm house, as well as elegance to the great mansion. The Early Texas house, with its row of posts across the front supporting a roof, was with very little effort transformed into a simple Greek Revival house. The builder had only to enlarge the posts or columns and add a few moldings or strips at the top and then surmount this with a proportionately heavier beam or entablature and top the whole thing with a simple cornice. Those houses which do not have fully developed classic moldings and orders, but whose proportions, forms, and details are based on Greek Revival models, we shall call "vernacular" Greek Revival to distinguish them from the true Greek Revival houses, which employ one of the classic orders or which display particularly sophisticated usage of classic moldings and classic proportions.

The Greek Revival, which was the second major architectural development of the nineteenth century in Texas, coincided with the ante-bellum or Pre-Civil War Period. It appeared in Texas in the 1840's and remained the major architectural style until 1870. Although the Civil War effectively terminated the style, a few examples built after the War reflect a stylistic lag which could be blamed in part on the isolation of the South following the War and during the reconstruction era. An especially fine post-Civil War or late Greek Revival example is the General Sam Bell Maxey House in Paris.

The Greek Revival is one of the first stylistic developments which can be considered an American (United States) architectural expression. Following the Federal style, which was based on Late Georgian or Palladian influences, the Greek Revival came into being as the first native expression of the new nation and, at the same time, the last manifestation of the preindustrial age. Because of its popularity in the ante-bellum South and because of many romantic literary associations, the Greek Revival style is commonly, but erroneously, referred to as Southern Colonial; although, as has already been pointed out, it is neither exclusively Southern nor is it colonial.

From the time of Austin's colonizing efforts to the Civil War, planters and planters' sons came from the Old South to Texas to establish the plantation system in the state. They were naturally drawn to the eastern half of the state, where they found good cotton, sugarcane, and rice land. Indeed, it is in Texas that the farthest extension of Southern culture is to be found; the cities of San Antonio, Austin, and Waco mark the western boundary of the Old South. There the Greek Revival style flowered in such final examples as the Vance House (no longer standing) in San Antonio, the Governor's Mansion in Austin, and the General Harrison House in Waco.

This last expression of the nineteenth-century classic revival is based on the form of the Greek temple, a gable-roofed rectangular building surrounded by a colonnade. Into this temple form were pressed houses, banks, churches, libraries, and schools. Although we recognize the beauty and sometimes the perfection of the form, we

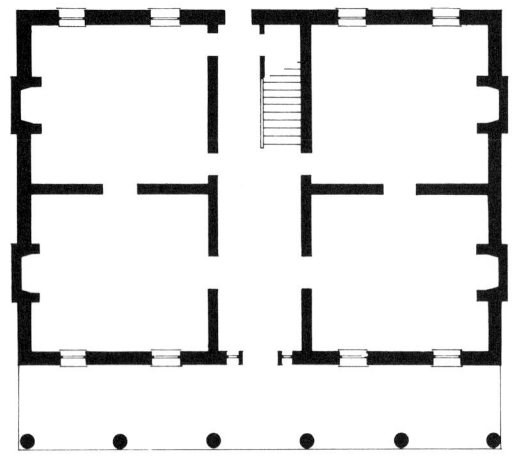

7. *Greek Revival House Plan*

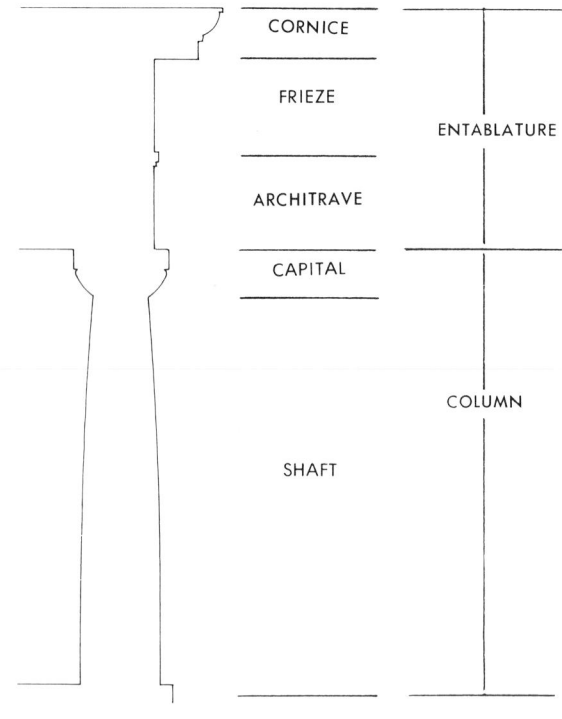

CORNICE

FRIEZE

ENTABLATURE

ARCHITRAVE

CAPITAL

COLUMN

SHAFT

8. *The Parts of a Classic Order*

must also acknowledge its limitations—its rigidity and its lack of adaptability to the many uses to which it was applied. Nevertheless, while it flourished—from 1820 to 1860—it provided this nation with its highest level of architectural achievement. As Talbot Hamlin, in his *Greek Revival Architecture in America* (pp. 315, 329), has written, "one wonders at its unity, its harmony, the quiet loveliness of so many towns, the restful serenity of so many houses and churches, the dignified impressiveness of so many public buildings . . . [It produced] an architecture alive, native, gracious, and sensitive, and towns that are delightful in their quiet harmony."

The Greek Revival builder in Texas (where there were few if any architects as we think of them today) used the Greek temple, a rectangle with a peristyle, or encircling galleries, surmounted by a gable roof, simplifying it and translating it from marble into brick, wood, and stucco. The Georgian house plan with its formal symmetry and the Early Texas house with its simple scheme were transformed into Greek Revival merely by the addition of the peristyle or columnar porch. This feature was usually carried across the front of the house, as in the Governor's Mansion in Austin, but in a few examples it was continued around the sides and even across the back, making the structure peripteral. The more classic examples had a low gable or pediment above the colonnaded portico, although this was frequently omitted. Another form used a central portico which framed and sheltered the front door but did not extend the full width of the front of the house. This form, although using orders and proportions derived from Greek sources, is Palladian in inspiration and comes down through Thomas Jefferson and the Federal style. It is best exemplified in the portico which was added to the north front of the White House. It could be of two or four columns, but if four columns were used they might be paired rather than equally spaced; a fine example of such pairing is the Swisher-Scott House in Austin.

The Greek Revival plan (Fig. 7), a central hall with identical rooms on either side, is a continuation of the formal plans of the eighteenth century and is the basic American house plan from 1700 to 1870 or later. It was the standard plan of the Georgian house in the eighteenth century, as it was the basis, in simplified form, of the double log house and the Early Texas frame house in the nineteenth century. Thus for more than a century and a half the builder did not concern himself with the development of a plan or room layout. The size of the rooms, the materials to be used, the proportions of the mass of the house, and the overall lines of roof and porch were the responsibility of the builder. It is to the good eye of men like Abner Cook that we owe the fine proportions and handsome lines of such houses as the Governor's Mansion and many other lovely Greek Revival houses in Texas (Fig. 8). The details of the columns, either Doric or Ionic, the window and door trim, mantels, and stairs were selected from the plates in builders' handbooks, which were published in great numbers at this time. *The Practical House Carpenter* by Asher Benjamin and *The Beauties of Modern Architecture* by Minard Lafever were two of the best known handbooks, undoubtedly serving as the source for many of the fine details in the houses of Augustus Phelps in San Augustine and in the Cherry House in Houston.

The Greek Revival lent itself admirably to simplification; its directness and boldly scaled detail could be captured very easily with a minimum expenditure of time and materials. This is what made the style so well suited to the conditions of mid-nineteenth-century Texas, and why

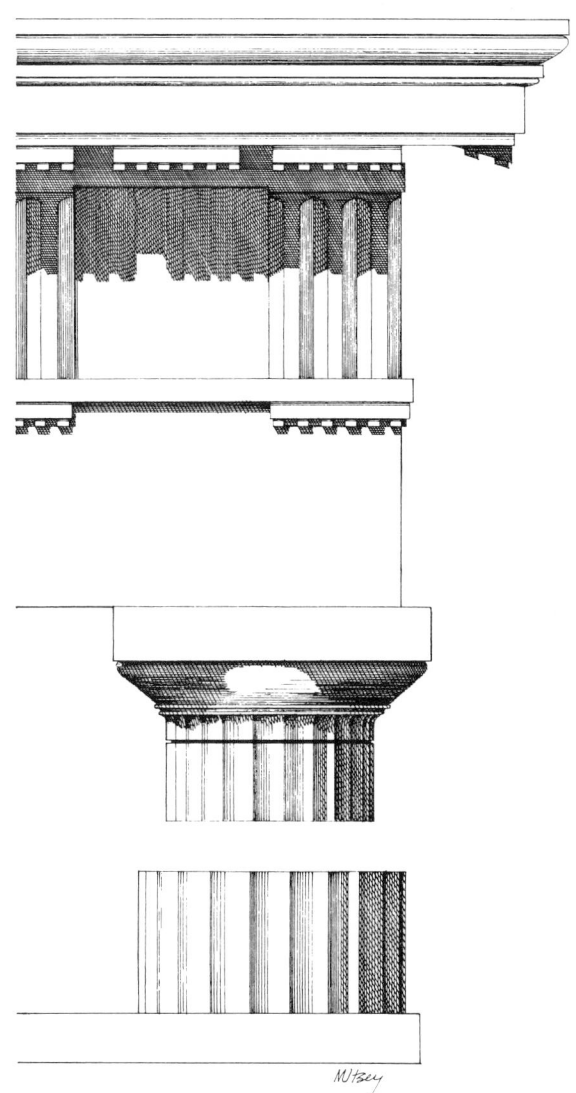

9. *Greek Doric Order*

87

10. *Greek Ionic Order*

it produced a gracious and dignified setting for a society which had a highly developed esthetic concern, strong ties with the established Southern culture, and very limited means for achieving its architectural aims. Because of problems of transportation, it was quite common for the builder to manufacture almost every part of the building on the site, with the exception of the hardware. Moldings were hand-planed, and even window sashes were often made at the site. However, in Galveston and other cities where shipping was no problem many parts such as columns, mantels, stairs, and even entire houses were imported.

The columns, the trademark of the style, were either of the Doric (Fig. 9) or the Ionic (Fig. 10) order. The more elaborate Corinthian was far too complicated; it demanded too much of the craftsman and too much fine supporting detail in its accompanying cornice, window, and door details to be practical in this new country. The Ionic, however, was quite often treated with finesse, as can be seen in Abner Cook's work in Austin. The Doric, which was the simplest and consequently most popular, ranged from the well-executed forms in the Neill-Cochran House in Austin and the General Harrison House in Waco, to the simple square posts, capped by a few simple moldings, which were common throughout the countryside in the eastern half of the state.

The treatment of windows at this time is fairly uniform in the consistent use of multipaned double-hung sash. Each pane of glass is called a "light," and each sash usually contained six or nine lights, with two sashes for each window. We often read descriptions of such windows as six-over-six or six-over-nine, meaning a top sash of six lights over a lower sash of six or nine, as the case may be

(Fig. 11). One good clue to the age of a house is the sash pattern. Of course, this kind of dating requires that the house still has its original windows, since windows and doors are so often replaced either because of wear or because of remodelling, that is, up-dating to a "new" style. In Texas the use of a sash with six or more lights is a good sign that the windows, and therefore the house, date from before 1870 and are stylistically of the Greek Revival Period. A sash with only one vertical mullion and two long vertical lights or panes is certainly post-Civil War and likely to be of the 1880–1910 period, characteristic generally of the Victorian style (Fig. 12). It is hardly necessary to point out that in the twentieth century the multipaned sash has been widely used in imitation of the Georgian and Classic Revival styles.

The cornice molding, the crown or cyma-recta (Fig. 13), one of the most beautiful forms in classic architecture, is at the same time one of the most difficult details for the local builder to produce. In place of this elaborate double-curved molding, the Texas builder frequently substituted a simple bevel, rounded off at each edge, which served very nicely for his purpose (Fig. 13). Simplifications such as this we see throughout the Greek Revival in Texas, and only in the most elaborate mansions can we find the full range of classic moldings.

Until the Civil War the Greek Revival in Texas remained fairly pure stylistically, simplifying the details found in the handbooks but never elaborating upon them or deviating from them. Following the Civil War the Greek Revival did not immediately disappear in Texas, as it did in the East, but changed in some aspects, the thin vertical line of the Victorian period gradually replacing the classic horizontality of the Greek Revival. Perhaps the

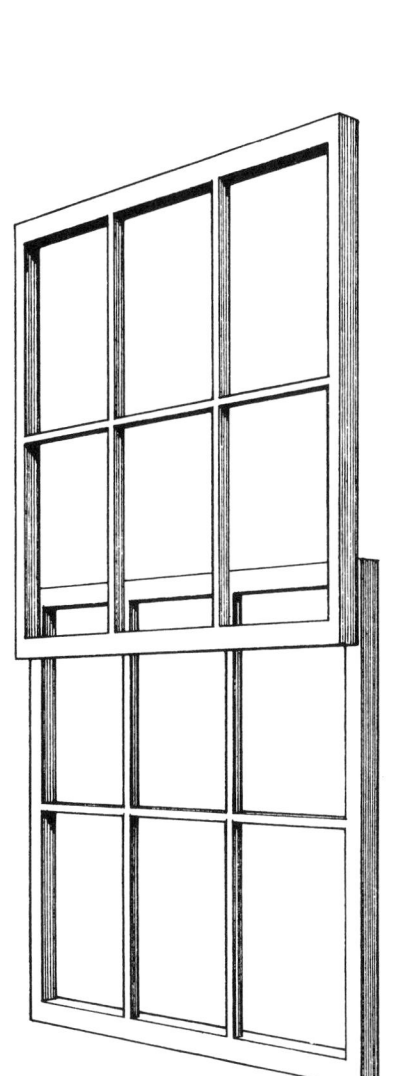

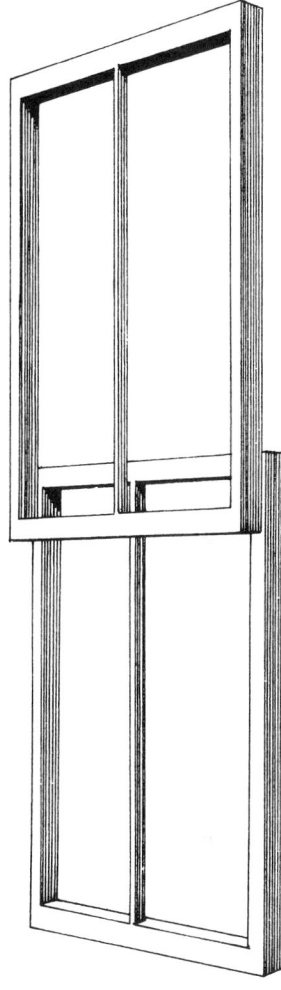

12. *Double-Hung Sash with Two-over-Two Lights*

11. *Double-Hung Sash with Six-over-Six Lights*

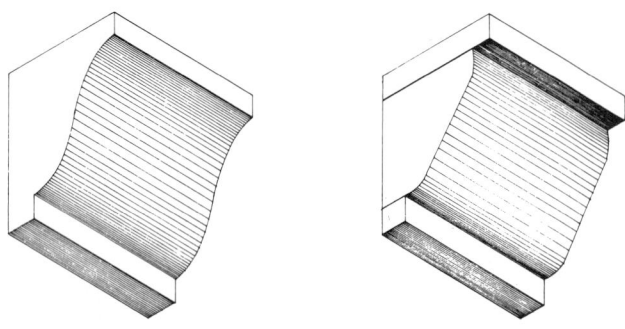

13. *Cyma Recta, or Crown Molding, and Beveled Molding*

first noticeable change appeared in the proportions of the windows. From 1870 on they became taller and narrower, with only the one vertical mullion in each sash, further emphasizing their verticality. As a result of the growing number of lumber mills and power saws, the classic detail became also more and more overlaid with jigsaw ornament. Classic restraint gave way to romantic enthusiasm for the decorative. The shift from Greek Revival to Victorian was not a sudden change, but a gradual development which produced some very charming hybrids. The houses exemplifying this double nature usually retain the Greek Revival symmetry of plan and the columnar porch, but the detail now has more of the flat pattern elaboration and the jigsaw-cut brackets that characterize the ornament of the 1880's. The combination resulted in many houses which have the dignity and grace of the classic and the liveliness of the more ornate Victorian style.

Because of a series of revivals of classic forms, based on the columnar porch, it is necessary to call attention to the problem of recognizing the true Greek Revival so as not to confuse it with the "Colonial Revival" and the "Southern Colonial." From 1900 until World War I the popular style for larger, more pretentious houses was "Colonial Revival," a term which, like "Southern Colonial," is a gross misnomer. "Colonial Revival" was introduced in the late nineteenth century by McKim, Mead and White and other architects who were building large summer residences for wealthy clients at Newport, R.I. The use of great classic columns, Roman Corinthian being the favorite, was further encouraged by the Chicago World's Columbian Exposition of 1893. This style remained popular in Texas through the first two decades of the twentieth century. During this time many Victorian houses were remodelled by the addition of a great two-story porch of Corinthian columns across the front. And later, in the thirties, a nostalgic interest in the Old South, spurred on by novels such as *Gone with the Wind,* made "Southern Colonial" the favorite style for large two-story houses.

These later revivals of the classic orders were usually more academically "correct" in the application of the elements of a classic order because in the schools architects were taught how to use the orders. The results, however, were spiritless and dull, and one has only to compare them with the true Greek Revival houses of the nineteenth century to see the difference between pretense and genuineness.

65. *Belle Air, West Columbia*

66. *The John Pierce House, Marshall*

67. Bluebonnet Farm (Tuscombia Ranch), Jefferson

68. *The H. N. Bell House, Bastrop*

69. The Meyers House, Jefferson

70. *The Cole House, Round Rock*

71. *The Colonel G. R. Howard House, Palestine*

72. *The Lockhart House, Chappell Hill*

73. *The Zorn House (Sebastopol), Seguin*

74. *The Petty-Killingsworth House, Hopewell Community*

75. *The J. B. Williamson House, near Marshall*

76. *The Drummond House, Hopewell Community*

77. *The Charles Bartlett House, Crockett*

78. *The Beriah Graham House, Austin*

79. The Columbus Cartwright House, San Augustine

80. *The House at 706 Rio Grande Street, Austin*

81. *The French Legation, Austin*

82. *The Horn-Polk House, San Augustine*

83. *The Sam Houston Steamboat House, Huntsville*

84. *The Old Stage Coach Inn, Chappell Hill*

85. *The Captain T. W. Blount House, San Augustine*

86. *The Griffith House, Montgomery*

87. *The Sublett House, San Augustine*

88. *The W. W. Browning House, Chappell Hill*

89. *Mont Hall (Edgemont), Marshall*

90. *The Andrews-Taylor House, Karnack*

91. *The Neinast House, near Shelby*

92. *The Collins House, Quitman*

93. *The Lee House, Independence*

94. *The Tait Town House, Columbus*

95. *The Wilbarger House, Bastrop*

96. *The Weisenger House, Montgomery*

97. *The Colonel Dewberry House, Teasleville*

98. *Liendo Plantation House, near Hempstead*

99. *The Baker Plantation House, Plantersville*

100. *The Henry Crocheron-McDowell House, Bastrop*

101. *The Schubert House, Giddings*

102. *The Schubert House (Door Detail), Giddings*

103. *The Colonel Basil M. Hatfield House, Washington*

104. *The Colonel Elijah Sterling Clack Robertson House, Salado*

105. *The General Thomas Jefferson Chambers House, Anahuac*

106. *The Callender House, Victoria*

107. *The Noble House, Houston*

108. *The Wiley Hill House, Hills Prairie*

109. *The George Evans House, Corpus Christi*

110. *The Oge House, San Antonio*

III. *The Hawkins Ranch House, Bay City*

112. The Williams-Tucker House, Galveston

113. *The T. H. Mathis House, Rockport*

114. *The Charles Stillman House, Brownsville*

115. *The Sedberry House, Jefferson*

116. *The Ezekiel W. Cullen House, San Augustine*

117. *The Stephen W. Blount House, San Augustine*

118. *The General James Harrison Rogers House (The Old Manse), Jefferson*

119. *Monte Verde, near Mt. Enterprise*

120. *Monte Verde* (*Door Detail*), *near Mt. Enterprise*

121. *The Brown House, Washington*

122. *The Cherry House, Houston*

123. *The Cherry House (Porch Detail), Houston*

124. *The Menard House, Galveston*

125. *Powhattan, Galveston*

126. *The Ball House, Galveston*

127. *The Fort House, Waco*

128. *The Napier-Kinnard House, Waco*

129. *The Matthew Cartwright House, San Augustine*

130. *The Judge Sebron Graham Sneed House, Austin*

131. *The General Thomas Harrison House, Waco*

132. *The Neill-Cochran House, Austin*

133. *The Swisher-Scott House (Sweetbrush), Austin*

134. *The Pease Mansion (Woodlawn), Austin*

135. *The Governor's Mansion, Austin*

136. *The Giddings House, Brenham*

137. *The General Sam Bell Maxey House, Paris*

138. *A House on Market Street, Galveston*

VICTORIAN ARCHITECTURE

THE YEARS from 1860 to 1900 fall within a cultural period known generally as "Victorian." The term *Victorian* as applied to architecture covers a wide variety of stylistic expressions which have been given such names as Queen Anne, gingerbread, jigsaw, General Grant, Mansardic, Shingle style, Second Empire, Gothic Revival, and Richardsonian Romanesque. The confusion of stylistic expressions is a reflection of the political, social, and economic turmoil of the period following the Civil War. The great expansion and development in these years can be compared to those of our own time with its equally confusing cultural and social upheavals and resultant architectural chaos.

We have until recently been accustomed to take a condescending attitude toward the Victorian Period, ridiculing its fussy detail and its overelaboration of forms. The "parvenu period" it was called, the era of the nouveaux riches, when the railroad and cattle barons, wanting everyone to know how successful they were, chose architecture as the means of showing their wealth. It is true that by our standards few great works of architecture can be credited to the second half of the nineteenth century. However, a more careful examination of the houses of the period will lead us to appreciate their charm and delightfulness, and to recognize the fine qualities of their builders: their love of rich material and detail, and the ability of many of them to achieve a harmonious composition out of the multitude of elements which made up the grammar of the Victorian style.

The Victorian style first appeared in Texas in those houses of the 1870's in which the earlier symmetrical center-hall plan was retained but the Greek Revival detail was replaced by the more elaborate and fussier Victorian ornament. This type might be called the symmetrical Victorian style. The porch was still the major feature of the facade, but in place of the classic Doric or Ionic column we now find the slender turned column. Frequently elaborate brackets on either side of the column filled the angles at the top where the column meets the beam.

The desire for a change from the boxlike forms of the past and the attraction of a new style led to the introduction of the Italian Villa or Italianate style. Flat or low-pitched roofs, a tower off center, deep bracketed eaves, and tall, thin windows and doors, which emphasized the vertical, are the characteristics of this style. Two early examples of the Italianate are the Brown House in Galveston and the Mann House in Waco.

Another style was the Mansard, sometimes referred to as Second Empire style because it was an adaptation of the architecture then in vogue in the France of Napoleon III. It is characterized by a mansard roof broken at intervals by dormers which are often round-headed. The roof quite frequently was enlivened by colorful patterns in the shingles or tiles and by crestings of cast iron or tin.

Following the post-Civil War transition period, which simply added elaborate jigsaw or cast-iron detail of a filigree character to the formal structure of the classic revival, we enter a period which reacts against the restrained formality of the symmetrical plan and balanced composition of the preceding two hundred years, adopting asymmetry as its basic principle of composition. No more do we have a door in the center flanked on each side by an equal number of equally spaced windows. Now, the off-center tower or turret is the most prominent element, especially in residential design. This can best be described as Turreted Victorian. At this time a more noticeable difference developed between residential and public buildings, which once were all cloaked in similar classic-temple facades.

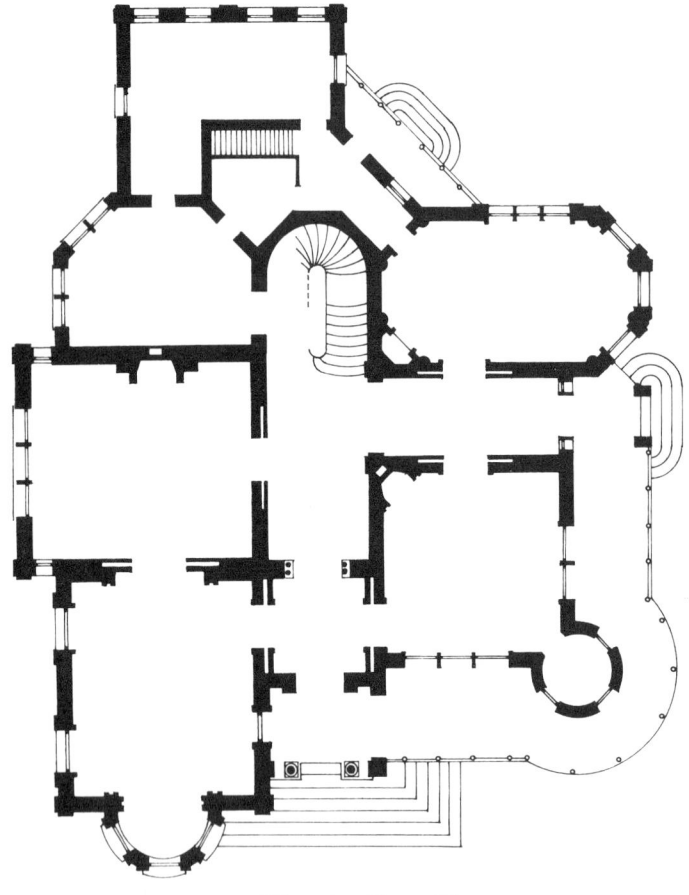

14. *Victorian House Plan*

Courthouses might still retain their symmetry, but residences were more and more picturesque in the irregularity of their outline. This asymmetry is characteristic of the larger mansions rather than of the small houses, which in many cases continued to be built with a central door, windows balanced on each side, and a porch extending across the front. The small-house type carried through the nineteenth century and into the twentieth century, when it became transformed into the American bungalow.

The Victorian Period was romantic in taste, and the architect or builder attempted to satisfy this taste by creating as "picturesque" a composition as possible. Instead of the simple rectangular plan of the Greek Revival, with its central hall and equal rooms on each side and its simple roof lines, the Victorian preferred elaborately irregular plans with as many bay windows, circular rooms, and angles as could be devised. The roof line was broken up with turrets, dormers, gables, and elaborate chimneys. The irregularity of form and outline, together with the elaboration of ornament and surface texture, provided the romantic quality so desirable in the Victorian home. As a means of expressing one's wealth or position, nothing could have served better.

The informal or asymmetrical composition of the Victorian Period was achieved by taking the old central-hall plan, bringing one room forward so that it projected out in front of the door, and then wrapping a porch around the remainder of the front and the adjoining side (Fig. 14). If the owner could afford it, there would be a tower or at least a conical roof with an elaborate needlelike finial at the tip of the cone or turret.

Among other things for which the Victorian house should be commended are its convenience and comfort. Although, when compared to present homes, the Victorian house could not be cited as an example of convenience, in it we find expressed many concepts which are essential to today's ideas of functional design. Once the rigid formality of the Greek Revival was broken, rooms could be sized and placed according to their use, and the more varied the sizes and shapes, the more irregular the exterior outline of the house might be—all to the greater satisfaction of the taste of the time. The idea of functionalism first appeared in this period when the purposeful use of the house and its spaces was considered in the development of the plan. What was even more significant, room arrangements were made according to logical relationships. The dining rooms were placed near kitchens, and kitchens were now in the house proper rather than in a separate building, as was so often the case in Greek Revival times. Plumbing and central heating were introduced into the more elaborate Victorian houses.

Expanded railroad service provided the builders with a wide variety of materials, and the desire for richness and variety in color and texture was satisfied. Brick, stone, tile, shingle, stucco, and cast and pressed metal answered the demand for variety; in many of the larger houses all of these materials might be found. In Texas the transition between the Victorian and the Greek Revival was perhaps slowest, for Texas then was still very much a frontier of American culture. There are few cities in the United States which have such a fine collection of late Greek Revival and Victorian houses as does Galveston. Here, where wood was a favored building material, the elaboration of detail is amazing. Turned balusters, spindles, pendils, and finials are to be admired on street after street bordered with houses of the 1880's.

From 1880 to 1900 cotton, cattle, and the railroads which served these products brought money and people to Texas. The major cities, Galveston, Houston, Austin, San Antonio, Dallas, and Waco, expanded. Tree-lined avenues led out from the bustling business centers, and along these main streets were the turreted mansions of the men who were building the state. The smaller towns, such as Victoria, Gonzales, Cuero, Corsicana, Sherman, Paris, the cotton centers of East Texas and the cattle centers of South Central Texas, had their share of mansions, which with the courthouses and the churches were the pride of their communities.

Certainly our greatest architectural riches lie in the nineteenth century. The Eastern States, with their colonial and Georgian monuments, until recently looked askance at the Victorian. In Texas, with the exception of a few major Greek Revival examples, our colorful past is best portrayed in such Victorian houses as the Gresham House in Galveston, the Littlefield and Bremond Houses in Austin, the Cameron House in Waco, the Waggoner House in Decatur and many others. The rich texture which they add to our environment is rapidly disappearing. Without the concerted effort of many people who value this legacy of our past it will be lost to us. The future generations of Texas, as a result, will have no visual contact with the past, and our cities will have lost the individuality that only unique architectural monuments provide.

139. *The House at 912 North Terrell Street, Cuero*

140. *The MacDonald House, Trinity*

141. *A House at Bowie and Walnut Streets, Columbus*

142. *A House at 16th and Post Office Streets, Galveston*

143. *A House at 13th and Post Office Streets, Galveston*

144. *The McNamara-O'Connor House, Victoria*

145. *The N. W. Faison House, LaGrange*

146. *The House at 602 St. Charles Street, Brownsville*

147. *The Moran House, Mason*

148. *The Kaulbach House, La Grange*

149. *A Row of Houses on Post Office Street, Galveston*

150. *The Shivers House, Woodville*

151. *A Gabled Victorian House, Shelby*

152. *A House at 13th and Sealy Streets, Galveston*

153. *A House at 13th and Sealy Streets (Detail), Galveston*

154. *The Brownlee House, Bonham*

155. *The J. H. Sturgis House, Waco*

156. *The Epperson House (The House of the Seasons), Jefferson*

157. *The Epperson House (The House of the Seasons—Detail), Jefferson*

158. *The George W. Fulton House, Fulton Beach*

159. *The Walter Bremond House, Austin*

160. *The Eduard Steves House, San Antonio*

161. *The Lay-Bozka House, Hallettsville*

162. *The House at 710 Houston Street, Crockett*

163. *The Daniel House, Paris*

164. *The Tinnin House, Georgetown*

165. *The John Wesley Mann House, Waco*

166. *The J. M. Brown House* (*Ashton Villa*), *Galveston*

167. *The House at 407 East Main Street, Clarksville*

168. *The Clein House, Cuero*

169. *The Ike West House, San Antonio*

170. *The Ashford Jones House, Nacogdoches*

171. *The Adolphus Sterne House (Detail), Nacogdoches*

172. *The Sonnenthiel House, Galveston*

173. *The Sonnenthiel House (Second View), Galveston*

174. *A Wooden Victorian House, Calvert*

175. *The Gruene House, Gruene*

176. *The A. L. Bowers House (Detail), Palestine*

177. *The R. C. Foitels House, Flatonia*

178. *The G. E. Dilley House, Palestine*

179. *The G. E. Dilley House (Detail), Palestine*

180. *The House at 515 Main Street, Brenham*

181. *A Victorian House, Calvert*

182. *The North-Evans Chateau, Austin*

183. *The William Cameron House, Waco*

184. *A Victorian House, Goliad*

185. *The John Bremond House, Austin*

186. *The Kennard House, Gonzales*

187. *The Collier House, Waco*

188. *The J. C. Trube House, Galveston*

189. *The Reynolds House, Mason*

190. *The Waggoner House, Decatur*

191. *The William H. Eddleman House, Fort Worth*

192. *The A. B. Scarborough House, Bonham*

193. *The Major George W. Littlefield House, Austin*

194. *The Gresham House (The Bishop's Palace), Galveston*

195. *The Gresham House (Interior Detail), Galveston*

196. *The Gresham House (Interior Detail), Galveston*

197. *The Colonel Edward M. House House, Austin*

198. *The House at 404 King William Street, San Antonio*

199. *The George Sealy House, Galveston*

200. *The George Sealy House* (*Interior Detail*)*, Galveston*

NOTES ON PLATES

1. THE JORDAN LOG HOUSE, near Huntsville

The Jordan Log House is an example of the one-room house with porch. Frequently to a single-room house such as this a second room and hall would be added later.

2. THE JORDAN LOG HOUSE (Detail), near Huntsville

This is an excellent example of the dovetail joint used in many of the log houses of Texas.

3. THE W. W. CRAIG HOUSE, New Prospect Community

This interesting log house has dovetail joints on the left side of the open hall and rabbeted or lapped joints on the right. The joints on the right corner are obscured by siding applied to cover the cracks between the logs.

4. THE CLAIBORNE KYLE HOUSE, near Kyle

This log house has two rooms on each side of the central hall, not arranged in the usual manner, with two rooms in front and two behind, all four opening into the hall, but with all four rooms and the hall in line across the front of the house, only the two inside rooms contiguous to the hall. There is a chimney between two of the rooms on one side of the hall and there may have been another chimney on the other side.

5. A RAIL FENCE ON THE BEHRENS FARM, near Bluffton

Fences, which enclosed house yards, pastures, and cattle pens, were a part of the pioneer landscape. The type of rail fence shown here was one of several which were commonly used.

6. THE WARREN LOG HOUSE (Detail), near Evergreen Community

Here is shown a rabbeted joint of a type in use during the early nineteenth century.

7. THE DABNEY LOG HOUSE, near Evergreen Community, San Jacinto County

In this view of the Dabney Log House the excellent log construction is clearly shown. This is one of the finest examples of dovetail joining to be found in Texas. The logs are unusually well fitted. Notice the one log which runs the length of the house and supports the joists for the second floor of this story-and-a-half house. The brick chimney, no doubt, is a later replacement of an earlier one, and the large nine-over-nine windows were very probably put in sometime after the house was built.

8. THE MONTGOMERY LOG HOUSE, near Cherokee

A good example of rabbeted log joints can be seen in the Montgomery Log House. Some chinking is still visible on the exterior of the house, and a fine stone chimney stands at the gable end.

9. THE DICK WEST LOG HOUSE, near Salem Community, Victoria County

This view of the Dick West Log House shows a good example of the stick-and-mud chimney, or cat chimney, which was common in the early days of log-cabin construction. Although not original (they required constant rebuilding), this one shows the method of construction very clearly—a timber frame to which is attached a small lattice or lath of sticks supporting the clay-and-mud cats which fill in the voids and cover the frame on the inside.

10. THE HOLCOMB LOG CABIN, near Moscow, Polk County

The carefully notched logs of this double log cabin and the sweep of the roof mark it as an outstanding example.

11. THE EGGLESTON HOUSE, 1300 Block St. Louis Street, Gonzales, 1840

The Eggleston House is undoubtedly the finest remaining log house in Texas. It has been restored with great care and now stands in excellent condition. The dovetail joints at the corners of the two rooms which make up this dog-run house are especially fine. The house is long and low, with the break in the roof slope accentuating the horizontal lines of the house, and thus giving it a strong visual tie with the land it sits on.

12. THE MILTON GARRETT HOUSE, 11 miles West on State Highway 21, San Augustine, circa 1830

Where the weatherboarding has been stripped off this fine log house, the joints of the carefully hewn logs can be seen.

13. THE W. H. LEDBETTER HOUSE, Albany

This is one of the few remaining examples of a picket house, similar in construction to the *palisado* house, in which the rough hewn boards are placed upright on a log sill to form the walls of the house. The spaces between the boards are then filled with mud, clay, or stucco. This type of house was not widespread in its use, being found primarily in the region of Ft. Griffin and in Shackelford County.

14. A LOG CABIN (Barn), Grenwell Farm, Llano County

This log structure represents a variation on the usual log-building technique. Here the logs, only slightly notched, are fitted with wide spaces between, unlike deeply notched logs, which may fit closely together. The spaces are filled with roughly shaped stones to form a log-and-masonry structure.

15. THE TURNER-WHITE-MAGEE HOUSE, Roganville, Jasper County

So well preserved is this house, and so perfectly situated, that it presents a most accurate picture of the Early Texas house. The tin roof, of course, is not original, and the balustrade is very likely a later addition.

16. THE THOMAS BARNETT HOUSE, near Rosenberg, 1836

The Barnett House is an example of the double-room house without the open hall or dog-run between. Without a central hall and entrance, each room has its separate door onto the porch. The double pitch of the roof is characteristic. The chimneys and porch posts are not original.

17. THE SAN FELIPE COTTAGE, Sam Houston Park, Houston, 1836

This Early Texas house was recently moved to the Sam Houston Park in Houston to be preserved along with the Cherry House and the Noble House as examples of nineteenth-century Texas architecture. Its simple form, a galleried story-and-a-half cottage, exemplifies the type of house that was built by the first Anglo-American settlers in East Texas.

18. THE RANDOLPH C. DOOM HOUSE, Bevilport Community, 1852

The Doom House in Bevilport is a good East Texas house, revealing its Southern heritage in the gallery, which stretches across the front and which is accommodated within the roof of the house itself. As was often the case, each of the two rooms along the porch had an outside door onto the porch.

19. THE SAM HOUSTON HOUSE (The Wigwam), Sam Houston State College, Huntsville

Sam Houston's first home in Huntsville he called the Wigwam. It is a good example of a frequent occurrence in East Texas houses—the gradual development from a one-room log cabin to an ample six-room house of a simplified Greek Revival form. The one-room log cabin was first enlarged by the addition of a dog-run hall and a room across the hall. The hall was then closed in, and other rooms were added at the back, as well as a half story above the main part of the house. Siding was added to cover the original log structure.

20. THE SAM HOUSTON HOUSE (The Wigwam—Interior of Hall), Sam Houston State College, Huntsville

This view of the interior of the Wigwam shows the wide hall which was made by closing the dog-run with a double-door, transom, and side-lights. By this means, the dog-run, which was a very comfortable living space in the summer, could be utilized as a livingroom in the winter.

21. THE CAPTAIN W. E. HEARD HOUSE, Egypt, 1849–1854

Captain William J. E. Heard was born near Knoxville, Tennessee. In building his house he must have recalled the fine eighteenth-century Georgian houses in Tennessee and nearby Virginia, for his mid-nineteenth-century Texas house is Georgian in its basic form. The same influence is obvious also in his choice of brick, which was not the common material of this area, and in such details as the twin chimneys in the gable ends. The porch columns and dormers appear to be later additions.

22. THE W. T. SCOTT HOUSE, Scottsville, 1840

This early Texas house was built in 1840 by William Thomas Scott, an early Texas patriot and statesman. Typifying the Southerner who settled in East Texas, he established a large plantation, first building log houses for his family, then replacing these with the large one-story galleried house which still stands.

23. THE JIM ODOM HOUSE, Cherokee Community

The Odom House is a representative example of the galleried Texas house, very simple in detail, with small, six-light sash in the windows. The brick foundation wall of the porch is not original.

24. THE A. GOLDMAN HOUSE, 107 South Liberty, Victoria, 1865

The Goldman House in Victoria is an example of the raised cottage with simplified classic detail and Greek Revival lines.

25. THE J. C. HILL HOUSE, Maynard Community

Settled picturesquely in its house yard amid moss-draped trees, this large story-and-a-half Texas house shows an elaboration on the form by the use of the two rooms at each end of the front porch. Such a room was usually referred to as the "room-on-the-porch." The tall gabled dormers and four light sashes suggest a late nineteenth-century date for this East Texas house.

26. THE SAGE HOUSE, near Starrville, Smith County

The Sage House is another example of the room-on-the-porch scheme, which, by closing the porch at each end, creates a recessed porch. Judging from the nine-over-six sash and the wide doors and sidelights which fill in the hall opening, this is a mid-nineteenth-century house.

27. THE MEREDITH-HART HOUSE, Rio Vista, 1856

In overall effect, this is surely one of the handsomest and most representative of Texas homes. In this house are combined the double gallery of the two-story Greek Revival and the lines and simplicity of the early double-room frame house. The result is a house that is straightforward Texan and that expresses both comfort and dignity. The central hall is entered through a transomed, sidelighted, double door. On either side of the central door the front rooms open onto the porch by smaller doors. This small-large-small door pattern is charmingly reflected in the column placement and the balustrades.

28. THE JOSEPH H. POLLEY HOUSE (Whitehall), La Vernia, 1840

This imposing two-story stone house was built for a New Yorker, Joseph Polley, who came to Texas as one of Austin's colonists. Its massive walls and generous proportions make it one of the most important plantation homes in early Texas. It was built for a far more spacious scale of living than was found in most early Texas homes. Although it does not have columns of a classic order, its wide double galleries are inspired by the Greek Revival style.

29. THE CAPTAIN NELSON MERRELL HOUSE, Highway 79, Round Rock, 1870

This two-story stone farmhouse has numerous features which give it an air of distinction. Among them are the balustraded cupola, the deep double gallery with finely turned balusters, and the long horizontal lines of the roof and gallery, which tie the house to the ground.

30. THE HUMPHREY HOUSE, Seguin

The outside stair and the two doors on each porch suggest a two-room floor plan with the access to the second floor from the stair on the porch. This is a type of plan frequently found in Louisiana.

31. THE JAMES B. JOHNSON HOUSE (Old Halfway Inn), 2 miles west of Chireno, the 1840's

A number of unusual features are found in this house. Perhaps the most unusual is the column, composed of three boards joined by a series of small wood spacers. The change in siding at the first floor on the front and the slight change in the pitch of the roof suggest that the present porch columns and roof are a later remodelling and that originally there may have been a one-story porch across the front.

The Johnson House received the name Halfway Inn from

the fact that it was used as a halfway station between San Augustine and Nacogdoches.

32. AN OLD STAGE-COACH STATION, Independence

This is one of a group of three similar two-story stone buildings which are referred to as "stage stations." Being of stone in an area where wood was the usual building material, they must have been buildings of some importance.

33. THE TENANT HOUSE ON THE DURHAM FARM, near Hamilton

Although at first glance this structure might be taken for a shed or small barn, the fine masonry, the chimney, and the doorsill, indicating a floor above ground level, all give evidence that it was built for living quarters.

34. A BARN, Austin Street, Mason

A significant adjunct to any farmhouse is the barn. Here is one which adds a handsome element of color and texture to its environment.

35. THE STONE WATER TOWER AT THE J. W. WHITE HOUSE, Mason, 1870

In the hill section of Texas, where stone is plentiful, it is frequently used for minor structures such as this handsome tower for a water tank.

36. THE KAMMLACH HOUSE, 309 West Main Street, Fredericksburg, 1873

The Kammlach House, now used as the Pioneer Memorial Museum, is a well-preserved example of German *Fachwerk*

construction with the typical form of a story-and-a-half with porch. The small casement windows, steeply pitched roof, exposed beam ends, and kitchen chimney rising from the lowest corner at the rear of the house are all German characteristics.

37. THE JOHAAN PETER TATSCH HOUSE, 210 North Bowie, Fredericksburg, the 1850's

This small stone house, dominated by a great kitchen chimney, has many characteristics of the Texas German style. The original portion of the house consists of the two rooms at the front, one of which has a stair leading up to sleeping space in the attic. The facade of the house has a decidedly German character, with its double door flanked by windows on each side. The walls, almost two feet thick, give a solid protective quality. The boldest feature of the house is the oversized fireplace and chimney of the kitchen, which was a later addition. The fireplace is about thirteen feet wide and has a raised hearth and a "Dutch" oven built into the wall.

38. THE HOUSE AT AUSTIN AND BOWIE STREETS, Fredericksburg

This little stone house is a very good example of the Fredericksburg Sunday house. Especially characteristic is the form as seen in this photograph, the small, high, block of stone topped by a gable roof with a low porch on the front and a lean-to at the back.

39. A SUNDAY HOUSE, Fredericksburg

This is a typical Fredericksburg Sunday house, an early Texas week-end house built by farmers who brought their families into town on Saturdays and returned to the farm on Sunday evening.

40. THE PETER WALTER HOUSE (St. Barnabas Chapel), 601 West Creek Street, Fredericksburg, 1847

The Peter Walter House was built in 1847. After serving as a home for over one hundred years it was converted, in 1952, into an Episcopal mission, St. Barnabas. The original half-timber construction, so frequently covered with plaster, is exposed under the protective overhang of the porch.

41. A DOOR DETAIL, Fredericksburg

The bow-and-arrow is a motif which appears in a number of transoms in Fredericksburg buildings, as seen here in a double door which is crowned by a fine cyma-recta moulding.

42. THE ADRIAN EDWARD CONN HOUSE, Blanco

The excellent masonry of this small house is representative of the quality of work done by German builders. Its form, a story-and-a-half, with porch, reflects the adaptability of the builder to the demands of the climate and locale.

43. THE ADAM SCHMIDT HOUSE, near Llano

The remains of the Adam Schmidt House reveal a *Fachwerk* structure with the heavy-timber frame filled in with stone masonry and then enclosed in weatherboarding. The house has, also, the typical German outline with a steep gable roof, which provided attic living space.

44. THE FALTIN HOUSE, Comfort

The disappearance of the stucco which once covered the exterior of this house reveals the braced timber frame, or *Fachwerk*, and its filling of finely cut masonry. This is a beautiful example of German craftsmanship.

45. THE JUDGE STIEHL HOUSE, LaGrange, 1854

This charming little structure is one of the finest examples of German *Fachwerk*, or half-timber construction, in Texas. Here the braced frame of square timbers notched and pegged at each joint is exposed, and the spaces between the timbers are filled with brick.

46. THE KREISCHE HOUSE, LaGrange, 1856

The Kreische House reveals the combined influences of the Germanic heritage of its builder and the climate and terrain of its location. The house stretches out along the slope of a hill with a double gallery across the back, providing an abundance of shaded outdoor living space. The construction is a combination of masonry and frame, both of which have strong Germanic characteristics in their details.

47. THE STAGECOACH INN, Winedale, circa 1835

The history of this interesting structure goes back to the 1830's, when William S. Townsend, from South Carolina, received title to the land and built a house for his bride. The oldest portion of the present building, a one-story, one-room house, may have been built at that time. In 1848 the property was acquired by Samuel K. Lewis, who very likely was responsible for bringing the building to its final state sometime in the 1850's.[1] The Inn reflects both Anglo-American and German influences. The room arrangement, with wide central hall and double gallery, is typical of the house type which the South Carolinians Townsend and Lewis would have known. The steeply pitched roof, small windows, and numerous structural details suggest that the work was done by German craftsmen. The column spacing on the double gallery is especially interesting in the way in which the columns reflect the door spacing—each pair of columns lining up with a door. The most remarkable feature of the Inn is the decorative painting found on the interior. In the upper and lower front rooms on the right of the hall are overmantel paintings, borders, and in the upper room an exceptionally fine ceiling painting done by a skilled artist. The ceiling painting is composed of Neo-Classic details—medallions containing symbols of the four seasons and, in the center, a green parrot. From all indications, the work was done by Rudolf Melchior, an artist trained in Germany, who came to Texas in 1853.

The Stagecoach Inn has been handsomely restored by Miss Ima Hogg of Houston and presented by her to The University of Texas as a museum and center for study of Texas-German culture.

[1] R. Henderson Shuffler, "Winedale Inn, at Early Texas' Cultural Crossroad," *Texas Quarterly* (summer 1965), Vol. VIII, No. 2, p. 134.

48. THE STAGECOACH INN (Ceiling Detail), Winedale, circa 1835

This detail of the ceiling of the room on the northwest corner of the second floor reveals the high quality of the interior decorative painting and the most remarkable feature of the building.

49. THE STAGECOACH INN (Mantel Detail), Winedale, circa 1835

This overmantel painting is located above the mantel in the northwest corner room on the first floor.

50. LANGE'S MILL, Doss

Lange's Mill is another handsome stone structure which reflects the German tradition in its square form and small casement windows.

51. THE PETER LANG HOUSE, Highway 152, near Castell, circa 1850

Castell was settled by a German colony in 1847, and the Peter Lang House was probably built shortly thereafter. Its compact, square, stone mass with the gable roof of double slope is distinctly Germanic.

52. THE DIETRICH RODE HOUSE, Cherry Spring

This massive stone house was the home of Dietrich Rode, first minister and teacher for the colony of German immigrants who settled at Cherry Spring. The great block, with its hipped roof and fine masonry walls, is a witness to its German ancestry. A house of this size, rising assertively out of the Texas plain, is an impressive sight.

53. DIETRICH RODE HOUSE (Barn), Cherry Spring, Gillespie County

On many of the farms of the German settlers the barns, as well as the houses, were of good masonry construction.

54. THE MARSCHALL HOUSE, near Prairie Mountain, Llano County

The Marschall House is a sturdy stone house of the late nineteenth century with a symmetrical plan and a few Victorian wood details. The arches over the doors and the keystone lintels over the windows are notable. The house was built by Otto Marschall.

55. A STONE BARN AT THE MARSCHALL HOUSE, near Prairie Mountain, Llano County

This stone arch is from a barn in a region first settled by German immigrants.

56. THE VANCE HOUSE (Landmark Inn), Castroville

This structure was first built as a home and store by Caesar Monad. In 1853 John Vance made it into a hotel and added the second floor and gallery. Its stone bathhouse was an uncommon feature in its early days.

57. KITCHEN OF THE VANCE HOUSE (Landmark Inn), Castroville

This small stone building is the kitchen of the Vance House and, as was often the case, is separated from the main structure.

58. THE CARLE HOUSE, Castroville

This combination house and store follows the European tradition of a shop on the ground floor with family living quarters above. In this case further details indicate the Alsatian background of the builder—such elements as the double, or French, doors opening directly onto the sidewalk and the covered balcony at the second floor.

59. A HOUSE IN OLD D'HANIS, Old D'Hanis

The form of this masonry house, a gable with lean-to at the rear, is an interesting copy in stone of a traditional wood house type.

60. A HOUSE IN OLD D'HANIS, Old D'Hanis

The fine masonry and small windows in this two-story galleried house reveal the characteristics of the Alsatians who settled this town under the leadership of Henri Castro in 1847.

61. A HOUSE AND BARN IN OLD D'HANIS, Old D'Hanis

This stone house with its auxiliary buildings reveals the harmony of a farm complex achieved here by the repetition of the forms—the low silhouette and the long sweep of the roofs.

62. A *PALISADO* HOUSE, Bracketville

In this simple cottage the ancient method of *palisado* construction is displayed. The stucco surface of the wall has fallen off in large areas, exposing the vertical posts which make up the structure of the wall. Also revealed are the reeds or twigs which are attached to the vertical poles and form the primitive lath supporting the stucco of the outer surface of the wall. This outer surface of stucco on lath is very similar to the ancient or primitive form known as "wattle and daub," a method of wall making in use since prehistoric times.

63. NORWAY MILLS, near Clifton, Bosque County

In 1853 the largest of the Norwegian settlements in Texas was founded by Ole Knutson in Bosque County. This handsome stone structure, both mill and barn, was built by Norwegians and given the name Norway Mills.

64. THE NOAH COX HOUSE, Roma

Although altered in some of its details, the Cox House presents a typical example of the Mexican influence on houses in the lower Rio Grande Valley towns such as Roma and Rio Grande City. Following the Spanish town house form of two stories facing directly on to the street, this type would often have a store on the ground level and the family quarters above, with a balcony, as in this example, for access to the open air. Frequently there were enclosed courts or yards at the sides or rear of the house. Of interest is the classic dentil cornice.

65. BELLE AIR, 2 miles east of West Columbia on County Road 703, circa 1836

This raised cottage, built by Dr. M. L. Weems, is a distinguished example of a type found in the lower South. The deep verandah provided shade and a porch high enough to catch any breeze. The broad sweep of stairs leading up to the verandah gives a handsome approach to the house. The dormers appear to be later additions.

66. THE JOHN PIERCE HOUSE, Marshall

This is a raised Greek Revival cottage with an unusual truncated hipped roof. Although somewhat heavy in its proportions, it benefits from the simplicity of its detail.

67. BLUEBONNET FARM (Tuscombia Ranch), Jefferson

Bluebonnet Farm is a representative example of the Greek Revival farm, or plantation, house of the mid-nineteenth century in East Texas. It grew from a log house built in 1847 by Mrs. Cutrier, who brought her family from Mississippi to establish a plantation here. Through a series of enlargements it reached its present generous size. Although it is one-story in front, the ground slopes down to the rear, where there are two full stories in an ell shape which opens on to a pleasant brick terrace.

68. THE H. N. BELL HOUSE, 1408 Church Street, Bastrop, 1850–1860

This early Texas home has its well-proportioned form sheathed in a charming and unusual fashion—the walls are vertical board and batten with the battens joined at both top and bottom by archlike cuts in the fascia. The square columns, treated in the same way, add harmony to the design.

69. THE MEYERS HOUSE, Jefferson

This view of a late Greek Revival house in Jefferson shows to advantage the use of latticework so popular during the second half of the nineteenth century. The charming summer house was often referred to as the courting place.

70. THE COLE HOUSE, Round Rock

An extremely fine example of the Texas house in stone, this building is particularly handsome in its broad horizontal lines and good proportions. Originality in detail, such as the column panelling, adds to the charm of this house.

71. THE COLONEL G. R. HOWARD HOUSE, Palestine, 1851

The fine proportions of this Greek Revival house show how successfully the Greek Revival form could be reduced and simplified in the one-story house. The corner pilasters and the columns supporting a classic pediment, the wide double doors, and the large windows are good characteristics of the vernacular Greek Revival.

72. THE LOCKHART HOUSE, 1 mile east on Old U.S. 290, Chappell Hill

Surmounting the Doric-columned gallery is a gable which houses a pointed Gothic window—an example of the free mixture of stylistic features which often occurs in the transition from Greek Revival to Gothic Revival or Victorian.

73. THE ZORN HOUSE (Sebastopol), Seguin, 1850–1855

This house is unique in many ways. It is a one-story raised house with a basement partially above ground and a T-shaped plan with a porch filling in the base and sides of the T. The stem of the T is a handsome drawing room or salon with French doors leading out to the porch on three sides.

Its second remarkable feature is the construction, an early use of poured-concrete loadbearing walls.

Finally, there is the panlike roof, which was built as a water reservoir to serve either as insulation to keep the house cool in summer or as an additional source of water.

At some point in its history the house has been given the name Sebastopol.

74. THE PETTY-KILLINGSWORTH HOUSE, Hopewell Community, Franklin County, circa 1858

This well-proportioned Greek Revival house was never finished, it is said, because of the Civil War. It was intended to have a portico at the front door, which would have given added distinction to the house. The details such as the window frames and interior moldings are especially good.

75. THE J. B. WILLIAMSON HOUSE, northwest 1½ miles on Road 449, near Marshall

Although a square post with a molding is used instead of a classic order, the refinement of details in this Greek Revival house gives it great charm and distinction. The dentil cornice above the windows and doors and the fine moldings used on the columns are especially effective.

76. THE DRUMMOND HOUSE, Hopewell Community, Franklin County

The Drummond House is an early Greek Revival house of unusual proportions in the height of the front in relation to the windows and doors. The treatment of the frieze and cornice is particularly interesting.

77. THE CHARLES BARTLETT HOUSE, 707 Houston Street, Crockett

The unusually large windows and door of the Bartlett House give it a grandness of scale that is seldom achieved in a house of its size. The two columns of the porch however are too small and have incongruous little brackets in place of a capital (perhaps a later replacement). The house is an excellent example of Greek Revival.

78. THE BERIAH GRAHAM HOUSE, 2605 Salado, Austin

This fine Greek Revival cottage has many of the characteristics of the work of Abner Cook, for example, the delicate wood balustrade of the porch, which is seen in the Governor's Mansion, in the Neill-Cochran House, and in the Pease-Shivers House.

This charming house gives us one more example of the variety that occurs within the small Greek Revival house type.

79. THE COLUMBUS CARTWRIGHT HOUSE, south on State Highway 147, San Augustine, circa 1838

This small house is a combination of the early two-room house and the Greek Revival house in that here the classic portico shelters two doors which open into the two front rooms rather than the single door opening into a central hall. Both doors and windows are unusually small for the house.

80. THE HOUSE AT 706 RIO GRANDE STREET, Austin

That the one-story Greek Revival cottage often achieved in its own way a degree of grace and dignity comparable to that of the large mansions is exemplified by this house. The proportion of column and entablature, and the relationship of column to porch, porch to house, and window to wall, were carefully determined to result in a satisfying composition. Especially handsome is the effect of the window height in relation to the door and wall. Instead of the present divided screen, each window originally had the typical louvered shutters.

The result in this case is a charming example of the Greek Revival which has been simplified in detail but which retains the proportions and the classic form of the larger prototypes.

81. THE FRENCH LEGATION, San Marcos and East Eighth Streets, Austin, 1841

One of the oldest houses still standing and one of the first built in the capital city is the French Legation, built for Count Alphonse de Saligny, the representative of France to the new Republic. The house has many French characteristics, such as the graceful outward sweep of the hipped roof, the dormers with their French windows, and the double or French doors opening onto the gallery across the front of the house. The gallery itself suggests a Louisiana influence rather than French. In the interior the French hardware, the doors, and some architectural refinements add a further French character to the house.

The French Legation has been preserved by the state of Texas and is open to the public under the auspices of the Daughters of the Republic of Texas.

82. THE HORN-POLK HOUSE, Columbia Street, San Augustine, circa 1854

The front of this house features two projecting gabled bays, which dominate the scheme, leaving the central portion with its porch as a connection between them. The result is somewhat reminiscent of the three-part Palladian schemes of American Georgian architecture.

83. THE SAM HOUSTON STEAMBOAT HOUSE, Huntsville, 1858

This quaint structure was built in 1858 by Dr. Rufus Bailey, whose idea it was that the house should look like a riverboat. Sam Houston bought the house on returning to Huntsville after his retirement from public office. Although built at the height of the Greek Revival tradition, because of its novel character it does not conform to any of the usual Greek Revival types.

84. THE OLD STAGECOACH INN, Chappell Hill, 1852

Built by William Hargrove and Jacob Haller as an inn, this house now has only the lovely Greek-key frieze to indicate its original classic charm. The porch, which at one time must have been supported by a good Doric or Ionic order has been replaced by a crude post shelter.

85. THE CAPTAIN T. W. BLOUNT HOUSE, San Augustine, circa 1854

This is a simple two-story house of a type that is distinctly Southern. A one-story portico shelters the wide double doors at the entrance into the central hall. A touch of refinement is seen in the shift from the nine-over-nine sash on the first floor to the six-over-nine sash on the second floor.

86. THE GRIFFITH HOUSE, Montgomery, 1876

The Griffith house is another two-story house of Southern characteristics. Its four fluted columns on the portico and the turned balusters on the first floor are likely not original.

87. THE SUBLETT HOUSE, 4 miles east of San Augustine on Highway 21, San Augustine, 1874

The addition of Ionic detail in the portico and the classic pedimented cornices over the windows together with the subtle change in size of the windows from first to second floor reflect the gradual transition of the Greek Revival style from the simple symmetrical house.

88. THE W.W. BROWNING HOUSE, Chappell Hill, 1856

The little town of Chappell Hill was an important agricultural and educational center during the Republic and the early days of statehood, and many fine homes were built in and around the town. One of the most impressive was the home of W. W. Browning, a large square block surmounted by a hipped roof, recalling some of the Georgian houses of Virginia. Its Greek Revival character is established by the pedimented two-story portico on the front and the colonnaded gallery across the back. Some of the fine details about the portico and cornice are now missing, but its form still reveals the quality in its design.

89. MONT HALL (Edgemont), west of Marshall on the Old Longview Road, Marshall, circa 1845

This porticoed, two-story, brick, Greek Revival house has the familiar hipped roof and interior chimneys of the Georgian Period. Its octagonal columns, however, are more typical of the Victorian style after certain medieval influences were introduced.

The house was built by Montraville Hall, and it is from him that the name Mont Hall is derived. It later passed into the hands of the Anderson family, who have given it the name Edgemont.

90. THE ANDREWS-TAYLOR HOUSE, Karnack

This East Texas plantation house is representative of a type found in the Marshall area—a two-story brick, porticoed mansion in a simplified Greek Revival style. The house was built by Milt Andrews and later came into the hands of the T. J. Taylor family.[1] The narrow Victorian windows are not original and do not conform to the architectural character of the house.

[1] Bracken and Redway, *Early Texas Homes,* p. 94.

91. THE NEINAST HOUSE, near Shelby

The builder of this late Greek Revival house took considerable pains with the detail in the cornice and columns. In this case a beveled crown molding substitutes for the cyma-recta in a very well-proportioned entablature. The great feature of this house is the painted interior, where pilasters, rusticated wainscoting, archivolts, and other architectural refinements are skillfully painted on the smooth board walls and ceilings in an imaginative effort to gain the elegance of panelling.

92. THE COLLINS HOUSE, Quitman

This classic brick house reveals the hand of a master mason in its fine flat brick arches over the windows. In addition, the proportions of the house, its central two-story portico within which is a cantilevered balcony, and the subtle distinction in the nine-over-nine sash in the first-floor windows and the six-over-nine sash in the second-floor windows, tell of a builder well acquainted with good Greek Revival practice.

93. THE LEE HOUSE, Independence

The Lee House shows the Greek Revival in its simplest form —square columns with flat plate caps and molding reduced to the absolute minimum.

94. THE TAIT TOWN HOUSE, Wallace Street, Columbus, 1856

Built by Dr. Charles William Tait as a town house, this late Greek Revival house was not completed until after the Civil War, when the two-story portico was added.

95. THE WILBARGER HOUSE, 1403 Main Street, Bastrop, 1842

A simple two-story portico frames the first- and second-floor central doors of this early Greek Revival house built by Josiah Pugh Wilbarger, one of the first Texas colonists.

96. THE WEISENGER HOUSE, Montgomery

A very restrained treatment of the classic two-story portico with four piers is the major feature of this early Greek Revival type.

97. THE COLONEL DEWBERRY HOUSE, 17 miles southwest of Tyler, Teasleville Community, 1854

Generous proportions and a fine two-story porch are the first things one notices about this East Texas plantation house. A typical feature of the porticoed house is the flush siding on the exterior wall within the porch, which contrasts with the lapped siding on the rest of the exterior. The extremely wide door, with transom and side lights, extends almost the entire width of the central hall and can be opened up to the breeze for comfortable summer living, a continuation of the open hall or dog-run feature of the early log houses.

98. LIENDO PLANTATION HOUSE, near Hempstead, 1853

Liendo is one of those generously scaled houses of simplified Greek Revival form which typify the Southern plantation house.

Built by the wealthy Leonard W. Groce family, it is more famous as the former home of Elizabet Ney, the sculptor, and her husband, Dr. Edmund Montgomery. The Montgomerys bought Liendo in 1873.

99. THE BAKER PLANTATION HOUSE, Plantersville, Grimes County

The Baker Plantation House has an ideal plantation setting, being situated in a fine grove of trees and fence-enclosed yard. The house itself is a very straightforward Texas classic. The two Doric columns and the front door appear to be replacements from a later restoration.

100. THE HENRY CROCHERON-McDOWELL HOUSE, 1502 Wilson Street, Bastrop, 1857

In the Crocheron House at Bastrop a classic two-story portico and well-proportioned windows result in a superior example of the Greek Revival style. At one time the house had an unusually fine cornice with a dentil molding, which provided considerable distinction.

101. THE SCHUBERT HOUSE, 183 Hempstead Street, Giddings

The Schubert House exemplifies the great variety to be found within the Greek Revival style. The corner pilasters with their quite original division of capital and entablature are reminiscent of corresponding features in some eighteenth-century New England Georgian houses, while the four-columned central portico has the lightness of the very late nineteenth-century Greek Revival.

102. THE SCHUBERT HOUSE (Door Detail), 183 Hempstead Street, Giddings

103. THE COLONEL BASIL M. HATFIELD HOUSE, Washington, 1854

This tall stately brick house set off by a white rail fence is a rather unusual type to be found in Texas. A two-story brick house is not often seen in this region, and its tall, thin lines, perhaps a clue to the origin of the builder, recall certain Virginia and Kentucky houses of a much earlier time.

104. THE COLONEL ELIJAH STERLING CLACK ROBERTSON HOUSE, southwest of Salado on Highway 81, Salado, 1856–1860

As an example of Texas plantation architecture, the Robertson House and its dependencies are unsurpassed. The use of gallery rooms which form terminal pavilions balancing the central gabled portico may have been inspired by a house in Tennessee, the birthplace of the builder. Although occasional examples of this form are seen in Southern plantation houses, it is unusual in Texas. The division of the facade into five parts, the central bay and two end bays forming pavilions surmounted by gables and separated by galleries, is descended from a Palladian form.

105. THE GENERAL THOMAS JEFFERSON CHAMBERS HOUSE, Cummings Street, Anahuac, 1845

This pleasant little two-story house, built along the lines of the Greek Revival, reveals in part the variety which occurred throughout the period. The deep overhanging eaves and lattice-sheltered galleries, together with the exterior spiral stair, suggest a Louisiana influence.

106. THE CALLENDER HOUSE, 404 West Guadalupe, Victoria, 1854

This galleried house is problematical in several respects. It is named for William L. Callender, who was not the original builder, but an early owner, of the house. Having had several owners, the house has been remodelled from time to time with a major addition having been added at the back in 1911. The front door is a recent replacement. The general lines of the house, however, reveal its early date and mark it as a good example of vernacular Greek Revival.

107. THE NOBLE HOUSE, Sam Houston Park, Houston, 1847
Built by Nathiel E. Kellum

The Noble House in Houston is one of the best Texas examples of the Louisiana type of galleried two-story house. It is built of brick, with the square columns of the first floor of brick also. The low-pitched hipped roof covers both the house and galleries in the usual Louisiana fashion.

108. THE WILEY HILL HOUSE, Road 304, 6 miles south of Highway 71, Hills Prairie, Bastrop County, 1854

Six square columns capped by a well-scaled classic cyma-reversa molding supporting the roof above the two-story porch constitute an architectural form which goes back to George Washington's first use of the two-story columned gallery at Mount Vernon. The Hill House, built by A. Wiley Hill, is marked by unusually fine architectural detail, as can be seen in the fluted pilasters at each corner of the house, the finely molded window frames, and the door and balcony treatment. The thinness of the columns and the vertical emphasis of the proportions are qualities of the late Greek Revival house.

109. THE GEORGE EVANS HOUSE, 411 North Broadway, Corpus Christi, 1849

In its straightforward simplicity, this early Texas Greek Revival house typifies the frontier adaptation of the classic forms. It was built by Captain Forbes Britton, who was a Mississippian and therefore familiar with the fine examples of Greek Revival in that state. The house was later bought by George Evans, whose family owned the house for many years. In 1949 it was given the name Centennial House to recognize its hundred years of existence.

110. THE OGE HOUSE, 209 Washington Street, San Antonio, 1860

This imposing Greek Revival mansion was built by the United States government as the residence for the commandant of the U.S. Arsenal. It is known as the Oge House from a family of that name who occupied the house for many years.

111. THE HAWKINS RANCH HOUSE, Bay City, 1852–1854

The avenue of oaks which leads up to this handsome residence immediately suggests Louisiana, the likely origin of the style of this double-galleried Greek Revival house. The columns of the gallery and the dormers may have been altered in remodelling.

112. THE WILLIAMS-TUCKER HOUSE, 3601 Avenue P, Galveston, 1838

Although the Williams-Tucker House has many characteristics of the Greek Revival architecture of Louisiana and the deep South—wide galleries and a low-pitched hipped roof with dormers—the house was actually partially framed in Maine and shipped by boat to Galveston. The gallery is supported by light Tuscan or Roman Doric columns, which are also found in Louisiana Greek Revival houses.

113. THE T. H. MATHIS HOUSE, Rockport, 1867

The Mathis House is one of the most beautifully detailed of the small Greek Revival houses in Texas. It is a raised cottage on a brick arched foundation and has a portico of fluted columns with fine molded capitals and a handsome bracketed and panelled cornice. The hipped roof gives added unity to the well-proportioned mass of the house.

114. THE CHARLES STILLMAN HOUSE, 1305 Washington, Brownsville, 1850

This home of the founder of Brownsville, Charles Stillman, combines the classic gallery of the Greek Revival with the fine brick building traditions of Mexico and the Rio Grande Valley. A feature of the latter is seen in the extension of the gable walls above the roof.

115. THE SEDBERRY HOUSE, Market and Henderson Streets, Jefferson

The outstanding feature of the Sedberry House is its beautiful cast-iron stair. This double stair, which curves out from the raised main floor of the house, is decidedly of a Louisiana influence. The front of the house is raised on a full basement, which gives the entrance added importance. The thinness of the columns and the emphasis on the vertical in windows, doors, and gable, are characteristic of the late Greek Revival.

116. THE EZEKIEL W. CULLEN HOUSE, Market and Congress, San Augustine, 1839

In the Cullen House the gable and columned porch of the temple form are used, this being the typical Greek Revival pattern. A heavy entablature and pediment or gable rests on only four Doric columns, widely spaced. Since most Greek Revival houses were wider than they were deep, the ridge of the roof was parallel to the front of the house and the gables were on the sides. In the Cullen House, however, the house is deeper than it is wide, and the gable faces the front, giving a true temple form. An interesting feature, perhaps not original, is the use of metal leader heads as decoration at each end of the entablature. A leader head is the connection between the gutter and the down spout, and as used here serves no practical function.

117. THE STEPHEN W. BLOUNT HOUSE, 501 Columbia Street, San Augustine, 1839
Augustus Phelps, Architect

This excellent example of the smaller Greek Revival house was built in 1839 by Augustus Phelps, an architect or builder, for Stephen W. Blount. Its central block flanked by low wings is a Palladian form which was admired by Thomas Jefferson. In the entrance porch and cornice a bold Doric order was used, the correctness of this detail suggesting that Augustus Phelps had in his possession one or more of the builders' handbooks which provided the Greek Revival builder with the proportions and details of the orders.

118. THE GENERAL JAMES HARRISON ROGERS HOUSE (The Old Manse), 211 Delta, Jefferson, 1839

Although this house was built by General Rogers, it is known as the Old Manse, having served the Cumberland Presbyterian Church in that capacity from 1903 until it was bought and restored by the Jessie Allen Wise Garden Club. This classic Doric porticoed house is unquestionably the finest example of the Greek Revival architecture in Jefferson. The elaboration of the door frame and the thinness of the Doric columns suggest that these handsome features are later than the date 1839.

119. MONTE VERDE, near Mt. Enterprise, Rusk County, 1855

This handsomely restored Greek Revival plantation house built for Julien Sidney Devereux reveals a combination of bracketed cornice and classic detail that is characteristic of the later phase of the Greek Revival style. The present colonnade of full two-story Doric columns is a recent installation, the original porch being a double gallery with two sets of columns, one for each floor.

120. MONTE VERDE (Door Detail), near Mt. Enterprise, Rusk County, 1855

This detail of a door from the interior of Monte Verde illustrates how successfully the simple Greek Revival details were employed.

121. THE BROWN HOUSE, Washington

This beautifully proportioned Greek Revival house is notable for the perfection and the restraint of its detail. The handsome rectangular box is surmounted by a low hipped roof, from which the double chimneys rise. A one-story Doric portico, with two paired columns on each side, protects the entrance. Extremely tall, narrow windows—floor to ceiling—give vertical contrast to the horizontal lines of the house. The ornament is restricted to the well-proportioned Doric portico and the modillioned cornice.

122. THE CHERRY HOUSE, Sam Houston Park, Houston, 1850

The Cherry House, built by General E. B. Nichols, had a succession of owners, one of whom was William Marsh Rice. The house gets its name from the E. R. Cherry family, who saved it from destruction in 1894. After having been moved several times, the house is now located in Sam Houston Park and has been restored by the Harris County Heritage and Conservation Society.

The house is especially noteworthy for its fine Greek Revival detail. The anthemion cornice above the door is probably the finest example of its type in Texas and must have been taken from a plate in Asher Benjamin or Minard Lafever. Although it is a small house, two-storied with side hall, its crisp detail and balustraded, truncated hipped roof give it great charm.

123. THE CHERRY HOUSE (Door Detail), Sam Houston Park, Houston, 1850

This detail of the Cherry House shows the more elaborate detail of one of the handsomest doors of the Greek Revival style in Texas.

124. THE MENARD HOUSE, 1605 33rd Street, Galveston, circa 1840

This Greek Revival house was built by Michel B. Menard, the founder of Galveston, about 1840. A two-story gallery across the front in the Ionic order gives the house its dignity and charm. Wings and additions were added later.

125. POWHATTAN, 35th Street and Avenue O, Galveston, 1847

This fine Doric portico of three columns is only a part of the original porch. The house, which was originally built as a hotel, was later moved and divided into three parts, the main portion of which is shown. The classic detail is exceptionally fine, and, according to Barnstone, the materials and columns were brought from Maine.[1]

[1] Howard Barnstone, *The Galveston That Was*, p. 19.

126. THE BALL HOUSE, 1405 24th Street, Galveston

The Ball House is a vigorous example of late Greek Revival with four Doric columns supporting an elaborate triglyph and metope entablature. The door is given an extremely rich frame with elements which are suggestive of Victorian detail. The two-story porch has four Doric columns dividing the front into three bays. In 1901 the house was moved and divided into two structures.[1]

[1] Dorothy Kendall Bracken and Maurine Whorton Redway, *Early Texas Homes*, p. 178.

127. THE FORT HOUSE, 4th and Webster, Waco, 1868

This is one of three Greek Revival houses built in Waco in

the late 1860's which bear such resemblance to each other as to suggest that they were built by the same person. All are two-story brick structures with an Ionic portico. The Fort House is the only one of the three to have a two-column central portico.

128. THE NAPIER-KINNARD HOUSE, 814 South 4th Street, Waco, the 1860's

A two-story brick structure with a four-columned Ionic porch, this house has a number of characteristics which link it to two other Waco houses, the Fort House of 1868 and the Clifton House of 1866. These houses all use the same form of Ionic, a fact suggesting that they were built by the same man or at least that the same hand was responsible for the detail. In this case the Ionic capitals are simplified to an almost two-dimensional form. The warmth of the local red brick and the naive detail give these houses a distinct charm reflecting the time and locale of their construction.

129. THE MATTHEW CARTWRIGHT HOUSE, 505 East Main Street, San Augustine, circa 1840
Augustus Phelps, Architect

Although known as the Matthew Cartwright House, this building was bought by Cartwright from Dr. Isaac Campbell in 1847. It is one of three houses in San Augustine which represent the finest early Greek Revival in Texas. All three houses were very likely the work of Augustus Phelps, about whom little is known. The sophistication of his designs suggests that he had received his training from a master of the Greek Revival style, most likely in one of the southern states. He must also have brought with him one of the builders' handbooks, providing him with patterns for the fine moldings and detail as well as the correct proportions of his orders.

San Augustine was first settled by the Spanish in the early eighteenth century. Anglo-Americans came to this site early in the nineteenth century, making San Augustine one of the oldest towns in Texas. Among the early Anglo-American settlers were a number of Southern families of means who brought with them a familiarity with the Greek Revival style that is reflected in their homes, among the earliest and finest examples of this style in Texas.

130. THE JUDGE SEBRON GRAHAM SNEED HOUSE, Old Lockhart Road, Austin, circa 1857

According to A. W. Harris in his *Minor and Major Mansions of Austin* (n.p.), the Sneed House was built by a mason named Simms and a carpenter named Miles Byrne. Certainly one of the handsomest masonry structures in Texas, its form, dominated by the connected double chimneys at each gable, is strongly reminiscent of the great Georgian houses of the Atlantic seaboard. The overall proportions and the size and placement of windows also add to the Georgian character of the house. The closed but still obvious sockets for porch beams, which can be seen at both first- and second-floor levels, indicate that a porch across the front was intended. The porch was never constructed, however.

131. THE GENERAL THOMAS HARRISON HOUSE, 809 South Fourth, Waco

Although marred by the partial enclosure of its great two-story porch, the Harrison House still retains a large measure of the dignity and grace of its fine Doric order and is one of Texas' finest Greek Revival houses. The house was built by Mrs. Eliza Earle Thompson sometime before the Civil War. Later it was acquired by Thomas Harrison, a cousin of Mrs. Thompson.

132. THE NEILL-COCHRAN HOUSE, 2310 San Gabriel,
   Austin, circa 1853
   Abner Cook, Architect

The Neill-Cochran House is another of Austin's prize examples of the Greek Revival style, and, like its peers, the Governor's Mansion and Woodlawn, is the work of Abner Cook. Instead of brick, this house is constructed of local limestone, gaining thereby an added measure of identity with its setting. The exposed native masonry provides a handsome foil for the six white Doric columns which form the two-story gallery across the front of the house. As in Woodlawn, there is a small balcony, with the characteristic Abner Cook balustrade, provided for the central door of the second-floor hall.

Although not as large as the Governor's Mansion, the Neill-Cochran House has the generous proportions and simple plan of the Greek Revival.

The house was built about 1853 for Green Washington Hill. Later it became the home of Andrew Neill; in the early 1890's it was purchased by Judge T. B. Cochran. It is from the ownership of these last two prominent citizens that the house takes its name. In 1958 the Neill-Cochran House became the property of the National Society of the Colonial Dames of America, in the state of Texas, who have preserved it and opened it to the public.

133. THE SWISHER-SCOTT HOUSE (Sweetbrush),
   Austin, circa 1855
   Abner Cook, Architect

This house was built in the 1850's by Abner Cook for John Milton Swisher. It stood on San Antonio Street in downtown Austin until 1931, when it was dismantled and rebuilt on a site overlooking Lake Austin. There it became the central portion of a residence for Dr. and Mrs. Z. T. Scott, who called it Sweetbrush.

The central portion was rebuilt to the same scale and proportion as the original. The Ionic columns, with their boldly scaled volutes, are especially fine examples of the Greek order. Here they are paired on each side of the portico, an interesting variation from Cook's use of the Ionic on the Governor's Mansion and the Pease Mansion. The balcony railing is of the same delicate cross pattern which appears on all of Cook's major works.

134. THE PEASE MANSION (Woodlawn), 6 Niles Road,
   Austin, circa 1853
   Abner Cook, Architect

Woodlawn is one of several major Greek Revival houses in Austin which reveal the hand of Abner Cook, the master builder. A beautiful Ionic order is used in the hexastyle portico, which is carried across the front of the house with freestanding columns rising the full two-story height. Two characteristics of Abner Cook's work are seen here: the lack of a pediment or roof above the finely proportioned entablature, and the very elegant balcony above the entrance. So light and delicate is the balcony that it suggests cast iron, but it is actually a very clever bit of surprisingly sturdy wood joinery.

Woodlawn was built in the early 1850's for James T. Shaw, who sold it to Elisha M. Pease. Because of the long tenure of the Pease family the house is known as the Governor Pease Home, although it is now the property of former Governor and Mrs. Allan Shivers.

135. THE GOVERNOR'S MANSION, Eleventh and Colorado, Austin, 1853
   Abner Cook, Architect

The Governor's Mansion is, appropriately, one of the finest Greek Revival mansions in Texas and one which can be compared to the best examples throughout the nation. Its scale is grand, and, as it sits on a terrace above the street, it is approached from below as though it were a great Ionic temple. The house was designed and built by Abner Cook, the master builder responsible for Austin's fine collection of Greek Revival houses. It follows his usual pattern of a hexastyle portico with a fine horizontal cornice line to terminate the composition; no gable, pediment, or roof is revealed above.

The plan is the classic one of a central hall with two rooms on either side and a curving U-shaped stairway leading to the second floor. Later additions have been made at the back to answer the requirements of modern living.

The interior spaces are gracious and hospitable, with high ceilings and good proportions. The doors, doorframes, and stairs—of a restrained Greek Revival design—are original.

136. THE GIDDINGS HOUSE, 204 East Stone Street, Brenham, 1879

This is one of the last of the grand mansions of the Greek Revival style, already reflecting the Victorian in its projecting bay and in the interior woodwork. An interesting cornerstone records the date of its construction and also the date of its restoration by the wife and the daughter of the builder. The exposed brick masonry of the columns, excellently executed, is a most unusual feature. The interior is Victorian rather than Greek Revival, reflecting the date of its construction. The impressive stair was shipped from St. Louis, where it was built.

137. THE GENERAL SAM BELL MAXEY HOUSE, 812 South Church Street, Paris, 1867
Anonymous Architect

This home, built by General Sam Bell Maxey (CSA) after his return from the Civil War, is an excellent example of the late Greek Revival with certain elaborations in architectural detail which presage the Victorian. The proportions of the house are especially fine, an almost square block surmounted by a hipped roof with balustraded top. Rising from either side are finely panelled broad chimney stacks. The mass of the house with its central two-story porch is Palladian, but the details of cornice, windows, and porch are more playfully handled; although classic in origin, they have a flowery quality that suggests the Victorian. An unusual feature of the house is the window treatment—elaborate bracketed cornices with a transomlike division of the exterior shutters. According to the family, who still retain possession of the house, it was designed by an architect from Milwaukee, Wisconsin, and material was brought by wagon train from Jefferson, Texas. The carved detail was done in New Orleans.

138. A HOUSE ON MARKET STREET, Galveston

On the narrow town lots in Galveston the Greek Revival house was often reduced in its symmetrical plan to one room and a hall across the front, a modification frequently necessary in northern cities. Although all of the other details seen here are good Greek Revival, what is left of the capitals of the octagonal columns shows a certain Victorian deviation from the classic form.

139. THE HOUSE AT 912 NORTH TERRELL STREET, Cuero

This two-story frame house is a good example of the symmetrical Victorian style with, in this case, a particularly interesting rhythmical pattern in the counterpoint of window and column spacing.

140. THE MACDONALD HOUSE, Trinity

This tall symmetrical Victorian house is a good example of the transitional period from the Greek Revival to the Victorian. Instead of two-light or six-light sashes, the narrow windows have four lights in each sash. The balustrade, like a folded paper cut-out, and the simple corner brackets at the posts are also Victorian. This type of house was very popular in the 1870–1880's, both in towns and on farms.

141. THE HOUSE AT BOWIE AND WALNUT STREETS, Columbus

In an age that loved patterned surfaces, the jigsaw provided a rich variety of designs. One example is seen in this symmetrical Victorian house. Many houses of this style have been given a coat of white paint in recent years, making the tracery of the galleries stand out in sharp contrast. In this example, although the colors are faded, the original values can be easily imagined.

142. THE HOUSE AT 16TH AND POSTOFFICE STREETS, Galveston

The Galveston townhouse of the 1870's is typified by this tall frame Victorian house on its narrow city lot. The touches of refinement in the columns and railings are also to be expected in this city of rich wood detailing.

143. THE HOUSE AT 13TH AND POSTOFFICE STREETS, Galveston

Here is an imposing galleried and gabled frame Victorian residence with charming column brackets and window frames. Although it is essentially of the symmetrical Victorian type, a slight variation was introduced into the design by placing the gable above four of the six columns.

144. THE McNAMARA-O'CONNOR HOUSE, 502 North Liberty, Victoria, circa 1869

This is a beautifully crisp example of the symmetrical Victorian frame house. A classic square box is surmounted by a hipped roof with dormers and is faced with a porch. The restraint with which the detail is used and the formality of the symmetrical organization of the door and window treatment, together with the repetition of the elegant arch over door and windows, give this house great distinction.

145. THE N. W. FAISON HOUSE, 822 South Jefferson Street, La Grange

This quaint Victorian structure is reminiscent of an old-fashioned valentine. Starting out as a good Texas house, it was then enriched by the addition of the Rococolike jigsaw detail, the most unusual part of which is that at the base of the column, which forms a sort of balustrade across the front of the porch.

146. THE HOUSE AT 602 ST. CHARLES STREET, Brownsville

Greek Revival and Victorian elements are combined in this house. The windows and doors are classic, as is their alignment; the porch and dormer are more romantic. The combination produces a charming hybrid.

147. THE MORAN HOUSE, Mason

In contrast to the delicacy of wooden Victorian houses, the Moran House plays up the qualities of its stone walls by means of the bold ashlar pattern of its masonry, using sandstone for the walls and limestone quoins and lintels for accent.

The symmetrical block of the house is enriched by a bracketed cornice and a light wood porch.

148. THE KAULBACH HOUSE, 351 Colorado Street, La Grange

This fine symmetrical Victorian house reveals the persistence of the balanced plan with two-story columnar gallery into the late nineteenth century. The particularly graceful wood arches supported by very thin turned columns are unusual.

149. A ROW OF HOUSES ON POSTOFFICE STREET, Galveston

Four variations on the two-story gallery are seen in this row of Galveston houses.

150. THE ALLAN SHIVERS HOUSE, Woodville

This exemplar of the symmetrical Victorian house now houses the Allan Shivers Museum and Library. Its double gallery is embellished with especially fine jigsaw scrollwork.

151. A GABLED VICTORIAN HOUSE, Shelby

A subtype of symmetrical Victorian could be labelled the story-and-a-half dormered or gabled Victorian. Here is an example of this type, which was once very popular in both town and country.

152. THE HOUSE AT 13TH AND SEALY STREETS, Galveston

Representative of Galveston's heyday, the last two decades of the nineteenth century, is this two-story frame Victorian. The two-story gallery, symmetrically organized, is a holdover from the Greek Revival and a feature which is most appropriate in the Galveston climate. In the better examples of Victorian frame houses, as in this one, the rich detail is subordinate to the columnar forms, reinforcing rather than obscuring the structural pattern.

153. THE HOUSE AT 13TH AND SEALY STREETS (Detail), Galveston

Elaborate pediments and shutters such as these are typical of Galveston's wooden houses of the Victorian era.

154. THE BROWNLEE HOUSE, 220 West 6th Street, Bonham

In vigor and boldness, the ornament on the double gallery of the Brownlee House surpasses that of any other example of the symmetrical Victorian.

155. THE J. H. STURGIS HOUSE, 1316 Washington Street, Waco, 1887

The fine detail in this beautifully maintained example of the early symmetrical Victorian house is handsomely set off by the simplicity of the brick walls. The shift to an emphasis on the vertical is seen in the tall, two-light sash windows.

156. THE EPPERSON HOUSE (The House of the Seasons), Delta and Alley Streets, Jefferson

Now called the House of the Seasons, this was the home of Colonel Benjamin H. Epperson, a prominent figure in the history of the Republic and early Texas statehood. The house is a beautiful example of the transition period between the Greek Revival and the Victorian. In plan and in overall form it is Greek Revival, as it retains the axial central hall with balanced rooms on either side and a columnar gallery across the front. Its detail, however, is Victorian, with certain Italianate characteristics in the tall round-headed windows, the bracketed cornices, the gallery, and the cupola, and in the use of the projecting two-story bay windows. The unique feature of the cupola, from which the house gets its name. "The House of the Seasons," is the use of glass of a different color in each of the four windows—red, green, yellow, and blue—which color the landscape remarkably as one looks out of them so that the red glass presents an autumnal scene, the green, spring, the yellow, summer, and the blue, winter. Another very fascinating feature of the house is the open hall well, which rises from the ground floor up to the cupola very much like a rotunda beneath a dome.

157. THE EPPERSON HOUSE (The House of the Seasons —Detail), Delta and Alley Streets, Jefferson

This detail from the Epperson House shows the circular well of the central hall which opens up into a dome above the second floor and which is lighted by the cupola above.

158. THE GEORGE W. FULTON HOUSE, Fulton Beach, Aransas County, 1872

The Fulton House is one of the most unusual and one of the grandest of the Victorian houses in Texas. The walls of the house, both exterior and interior, rest on a concrete foundation, and are constructed of one-inch-by-ten-inch pine boards stacked horizontally one on the other and pinned by stamped spikes. Each wall is a solid ten inches of laminated wood. The heating, ventilating, and plumbing systems were far in advance of the times and reflect the ingenuity of Mr. Fulton, who possessed an inventive nature similar to that of his cousin, Robert Fulton of steamboat fame. The house is of a fine turreted Victorian design with mansard roof and an asymmetrical composition.

159. THE WALTER BREMOND HOUSE, 409 W. 8th Street, Austin
George Fiegel, Contractor

The Walter Bremond House is a mansard-roofed stone structure with fine decorative iron work providing a contrast to the simplicity of the masonry. The house has certain similarities to the townhouses which were built in New Orleans and Savannah, where French influences were strongest. The most obvious similarities are the placement of the house near the sidewalk, the high, narrow proportions, and the dormered mansard roof.

160. THE EDUARD STEVES HOUSE, 509 King William Street, San Antonio, 1876

King William Street in San Antonio still maintains an aura of wealth and Victorian ostentation that recalls the period following the Civil War, when the leading families were building their mansions on a street intended to become a grand avenue. It was during this time that the Steves House was built. It is a symmetrical Victorian house with a mansard roof and Italianate detail, all blended into a fairly harmonious design. The house, with much of its interior furnishings intact, passed from the Steves family into the hands of the San Antonio Conservation Society, which maintains it as a museum.

161. THE LAY-BOZKA HOUSE, Highway 90A, Hallettsville, 1878
B. J. E. Deitz, Builder

This mansarded Victorian house captures the fancy of many
passersby. A part of its charm is the freedom with which a
variety of detail has been combined. The patterning of the
shingles on the mansard roof, which used to be such a colorful
feature of Victorian houses, is now quite rare, because of the
replacement of so many of the original shingle roofs. Also
interesting is the rope molding at the cornice of the dormer
windows and at the crown of the roof. The house was constructed for Dr. James E. Lay by B. J. E. Deitz.

162. THE HOUSE AT 710 HOUSTON STREET, Crockett

This frame house is a charming example of the mansard-
roofed Victorian style. The original patterned shingles, still in
place, were undoubtedly accentuated, when new, by a colorful
stain.

163. THE CAPTAIN J. M. DANIEL HOUSE, 216 4th
Southwest, Paris, 1876

Thin columns and elegant arches give distinction to the porch
of this early Texas Victorian house in Paris. A characteristic
mansard-roofed tower, hidden by the tree at the right, adds the
desired asymmetrical element to this nineteenth-century
"villa."

164. THE TINNIN HOUSE, 1220 Austin Street, Georgetown

In Georgetown is found one of the simplest statements of the
asymmetrical Victorian style, with a tower on one side and a
typical Victorian bay window terminating the composition on
the other. The porch and front door are not original.

165. THE JOHN WESLEY MANN HOUSE, Mill Street,
Waco, 1867

The Mann House, known as East Terrace, was built in 1867
of local brick. It is an unusually early example for Texas of
the so-called Italian Villa style, which had become fashion-
able in the East in the 1850's, but which was not generally
found in Texas before 1880. This is a house of many wings, its
thin vertical proportions accentuated by the tall windows,
mansard-roofed tower, and light galleries. The builder was
familiar with the new architectural trends in the East, where
there were numerous prototypes for this style, one of the
better known being the Wyman Villa in Baltimore, designed
by Richard Upjohn in 1851, which had many similarities to
the Mann House.

166. THE J. M. BROWN HOUSE (Ashton Villa), 2328
Broadway, Galveston, 1858

When J. M. Brown, a successful Galveston merchant, built
his home in 1858, he chose a style which had become popular
in the East but which would not supplant the Greek Revival
in Texas until after the Civil War. The Italianate, or Italian
Villa, style is a subdivision of the Victorian, and, like so many
of the Victorian styles, it has very little to do with the
influences implied by its name—either villas or Italy. Its
characteristics as seen in the Brown House are very low roofs,
deep-bracketed eaves, and tall narrow windows and doors.

A mansion of this importance, built in a new style, must
have created quite a stir in Galveston, a city which found the
Greek Revival style so congenial. The Brown House was one

of the first houses of any significance to introduce the new style to Texas.

167. THE HOUSE AT 407 EAST MAIN STREET, Clarksville

The fringed fascia, or barge boards, of the gables and the bracketed eaves inevitably suggest to the style hunter a Swiss chalet. However, this lacy detail was just a part of the jigsaw vocabulary of the Victorian builder. The columns of the porch are evidently replacements, for the original columns would have been thinner and more elaborate, like the pilaster of the porch wall at the left corner.

168. THE CLEIN HOUSE, 218 North Terrell, Cuero

Very often houses such as this are described as in the Swiss Chalet style. Certainly something of Bavarian or Swiss architecture is in the pierced work of the balustrades and the gable work as well as in the window heads.

169. THE IKE WEST HOUSE, 422 King William Street, San Antonio

This turreted Victorian house also happens to be symmetrical, at least from the front, as the central porch and turret are flanked by identical bays on each side.

170. THE ASHFORD JONES HOUSE, Nacogdoches

The inventiveness and exuberance of the Victorian builder, especially in wood, is displayed in the porch treatment of this elaborate frame house. Particularly delightful is the small pulpitlike bay which divides the front steps and centers on the double doors of the entrance. The beads and spindles are a feature found both inside and out in many houses of this period.

171. THE ADOLPHUS STERNE HOUSE (Detail), Nacogdoches

The washstand, a familiar Victorian amenity.

172. THE SONNENTHIEL HOUSE, 1826 Avenue I, Galveston, 1887

The fertile imagination of the designer (in this case unknown) was given free reign in the development of the wood detail on this wedding cake of a house. The unmistakable character of the French Second Empire style is in the look of the gables and cornices, as well as of the columns and pilasters. Below the bracketed cornice, however, begins the lattice work of an entirely different character, reminiscent of the *treillage* or trellis work found on French houses of an earlier date.

173. THE SONNENTHIEL HOUSE (Second View), 1826 Avenue I, Galveston, 1887

Here is a second view of the facade of the Sonnenthiel House.

174. A WOODEN VICTORIAN HOUSE, Calvert

Abacuslike are the beads and spindles which trim the galleries of this good Victorian house.

175. THE GRUENE HOUSE, Gruene, Comal County

Wood in the hands of a Victorian craftsman took many forms.

In this instance it was worked into a wonderful shuttered belvedere at the corner of the second-floor gallery, an ideal retreat for hot summer days.

176. THE A. L. BOWERS HOUSE (Detail), South Magnolia and Gooch Streets, Palestine

Vines, peeling paint, and stained glass add to the romantic quality of this detail of a Victorian house and also suggest the quality of the original colors, which invariably were rich earth tones—yellows, reds, and browns.

177. THE R. C. FOITELS HOUSE, Flatonia
Will Allen, Builder

For privacy, shade, and a place to catch a breeze, nothing is better than a latticed back porch such as this one from the late nineteenth century.

178. THE G. E. DILLEY HOUSE, 805 South Sycamore Street, Palestine, 1875

The G. E. Dilley House is a beautifully restored example of a large late Victorian house. The fine detail of the interior woodwork is especially notable.

179. THE G. E. DILLEY HOUSE (Detail), 805 South Sycamore Street, Palestine, 1875

This view of the Dilley House shows the carefully detailed porch, a favorite summer retreat of the Victorian era.

180. THE HOUSE AT 515 MAIN STREET, Brenham

The fascinating geometry of this turreted Victorian house is emphasized by the circles and triangles in its galleries.

181. A VICTORIAN HOUSE, Calvert

This late nineteenth-century house exhibits the playfulness of the Victorian designer and the multitude of elements at his command. The wonderfully inventive form of the wrap-around chimney and the domelike turret are instances of a stylistic expression which has been called Queen Anne, another name to add to the confused array of subdivisions within the Victorian style.

182. THE NORTH-EVANS CHATEAU, Austin
Alfred Giles, Architect

An interesting feature of this picturesque Victorian house is that it was originally a two-story symmetrical house begun in the 1880's. After a remodelling, completed in the 1890's, the house acquired a strong Richardsonian Romanesque character, especially in its porch details.

183. THE WILLIAM CAMERON HOUSE, 1223 Austin Avenue, Waco, 1879

The William Cameron House in Waco is one of the great Texas Victorian houses, standing with the Gresham House in Galveston, the Littlefield House in Austin, and the Waggoner House in Decatur as a monument to an age and an entrepreneur. A frame house, built by a lumberman and marked by elaborate wood detail, it reflects the taste of the time and the interests of the builder.

184. A VICTORIAN HOUSE, Goliad

This turreted Victorian house has all of the elements of its style, angular turrets, galleries, and asymmetry.

185. THE JOHN BREMOND HOUSE, 7th and Guadalupe
Streets, Austin, 1886
George Fiegel, Contractor

Although this fine Victorian mansion does not have the usual turret or spire, it does have a most elaborate gable, which reflects in its outward sweeping lines the mansard roof so much admired in the Victorian Period. The cast-iron railings and cresting on the house are among the finest to be seen in Texas.

This house is one of an entire block of family houses dating from the 1880's and forming one of the most complete Victorian neighborhoods still in existence in Texas.

186. THE KENNARD HOUSE, St. Lawrence and Hamilton
Streets, Gonzales

An extremely rich and fanciful example of the Queen Anne or Shingle style from the Victorian era is the Kennard House. The house boasts a central portico of two stories, the lower consisting of two Romanesque arches which support the light columnar gallery of the second level. This is surmounted by a pediment, which is covered with a bright mosaic of pottery and glass fragments and is opened by a Palladian window. This central portico is then flanked on one side by a bold turreted bay and on the other by a one-story gallery which wraps around the corner of the house.

187. THE COLLIER HOUSE, 715 South 4th Street, Waco,
circa 1867

It is unusual to find a one-story Victorian house with the pretensions of the grand mansion that are seen here. This is its charm.

188. THE J. C. TRUBE HOUSE, 1627 Avenue I, Galveston,
1890
Alfred Muller, Architect

The Trube House could very well be called the most fantastic of the Victorian houses in Texas. From the hooded dormers in the mansard roof to the multitude of motifs which cover each surface, every feature adds to the wonder of this most eclectic of designs.

189. THE REYNOLDS HOUSE, Mason, 1887

Now known as the Reynolds House, this home was built by Thomas Broad in 1887. As originally built it was a two-story masonry house. In this form it was sold to F. W. Henderson, who in turn sold it to Edward M. Reynolds. Mr. Reynolds enlarged the house to its present form by adding a third story and galleries. Although the galleries and turrets were apparently added to the house shortly after the turn of the century, it remains in form and fabric a fine example of nineteenth-century Victorian architecture. The house passed into the hands of the Oscar Seaquist family in 1919.

190. THE WAGGONER HOUSE, Decatur, circa 1884

This impressive masonry Victorian house was the home of the Waggoner family, prominent in the early days of ranching in Texas. In the boldness of the forms and in the strength of the material the builder achieved an appropriate expression for the client and the times.

191. THE WILLIAM H. EDDLEMAN HOUSE, Fort Worth

The spikey grandeur of this brick-and-stone mansion, representative of many fine houses built on the bluff overlooking Fort Worth at the end of the century, reflects the growing importance of that city as the center of the important cattle industry. The detail of the Eddleman House is exceptionally fine. It is a turreted late Victorian example, with numerous classic details characteristic of that era.

192. THE A. B. SCARBOROUGH HOUSE, Bonham

In Bonham is one of the largest and best preserved of the frame, turreted Victorian houses in Texas. In contrast to the earlier, thin, jigsaw Victorian, its forms are bold and massive and its galleries generous. This house displays many classic motifs, such as the columns, the bracketed cornice, the scrollwork in the gables, and the anthemion frieze of the turret—all forerunners of the Colonial Revival which was to follow in the 1900's.

193. THE MAJOR GEORGE W. LITTLEFIELD HOUSE, 24th Street, Austin, 1893
James Wahrenberger, Architect

The Littlefield home is a first-class example of the exuberance of the late Victorian. Because of the mansard roof and other details, it is often referred to as Second Empire style, but the variety of motifs would make any style designation other than Victorian difficult, if not impossible. In a neighborhood which once abounded in Grand Victorian mansions, the Littlefield House is now the only one left. Here is the typical Victorian scheme of a central entrance flanked by a bay-windowed, projecting parlor on the left and a gallery extending from the entrance around to the right, the righthand corner being a turreted circular bay. The color of the Littlefield House is red, a dark earth red, and Major Littlefield ordered a red sandstone for the window and door trim to match the red of the brick. The joints of the brickwork, pointed with a tooled marble-dust mortar, are extremely fine. In addition to brick and sandstone, granite, limestone, tile, slate, and iron were used on the exterior. A considerable variety of woods and tooled leather were used in the panelling on the interior.

Although there are numerous bay windows and projections, the plan is basically a central hall with rooms on either side. In this house an intersection of the wide central hall in the center by a crosshall creates on both the first and second floor a wonderful living space which must have been especially pleasant in the summer.

194. THE GRESHAM HOUSE (The Bishop's Palace), 1402 Broadway, Galveston, 1888–1892
Nicholas J. Clayton, Architect

The Colonel Walter Gresham House, perhaps better known as the Bishop's Palace, is the finest example of the turreted Victorian mansion in Texas. The house was designed by Nicholas J. Clayton, a Galveston architect who had achieved a considerable reputation in Texas and the South as the designer of numerous schools, churches, and fine residences.

The house, built of granite, limestone, and red sandstone, follows the usual Victorian composition of a central entrance flanked by a projecting bay window on the left and a gallery encircling a turreted tower on the right. This three-part composition is treated in the richest possible manner with not a plain surface to be seen anywhere. Despite the elaboration of detail, the boldness of the volumetric forms provides strength for this grand composition. The interior is impressively detailed with panelling and a grand staircase of many fine woods fabricated in Cincinnati. The detail of the house is much more original than one usually finds in the Victorian eclecticism of the day, revealing in Clayton an inventiveness which marks him as a designer worthy of further study.

The house was purchased by the late Christopher E. Byrne, Bishop of Galveston, in 1923, and, although no longer used as the bishop's residence, is popularly known as the Bishop's Palace.

195. THE GRESHAM HOUSE (Interior Detail), 1402 Broadway, Galveston, 1888–1892

This interior of the Gresham house shows the richness of the woodwork in this grand Victorian mansion.

196. THE GRESHAM HOUSE, 1402 Broadway, Galveston, 1888–1892

A cupola terminates the stairwell in the Gresham House.

197. THE COLONEL EDWARD M. HOUSE HOUSE, 1704 West Avenue, Austin, 1891
Frank Freeman, Architect

Colonel House, one of the most interesting personalities of his time and a figure of considerable importance in President Wilson's Administration, obtained the services of a New York architect when he built his Austin residence in 1891. Frank Freeman, whose work Colonel House had seen and admired in New York, was one of a group of architects who were influenced by Henry Hobson Richardson, one of the most important architects of the late nineteenth century. It was from Richardson and his school that the pioneers of modern architecture sprang. Because of the influence of Richardson and his use of the rich masonry forms of a medieval style, the architecture of this school is called Richardsonian

Romanesque. The house, which Freeman designed for Colonel House, is perhaps Texas' finest example of the style. Although based on an historic style, the significance of this work lies in the creative handling of forms and space and the love of fine materials naturally expressed. Because of the architects' concern for materials and their facility in the use of wood, especially shingles, the term Shingle style is often applied to the residential work of this school. Shingle style would, no doubt, be a better label for the House house, for in contrast to the Victorian style, the emphasis here is on the composition of the masses which express the interior spaces of the house rather than on the elaboration of decorative detail. This is accomplished by the bold use of masonry (red sandstone) and the powerful forms of the shingle roof which sweep out over the many porches.

The plan, too, is significant in its innovations. Here is an excellent example of the open plan, suites of rooms opening together to form spaces of great flexibility, with many openings onto the large enclosing verandahs.

198. THE HOUSE AT 404 KING WILLIAM STREET, San Antonio

One of the styles that followed the Victorian was the Colonial Revival, which became very popular in Texas after the turn of the century. It was introduced in certain sophisticated Eastern cities, such as Newport, R.I., in the 1880's, and it is possible that this example of the style from King William Street in San Antonio is one of the earliest to be built in Texas. Except for the Victorian proportions of the two-over-two window sash, the architectural detail is unusually good classic in the Corinthian mode. The house bears a strong resemblance to the Vassall-Longfellow house in Cambridge, Massachusetts, built about one hundred fifty years earlier, which reveals the persistence of the American Georgian style.

199. THE GEORGE SEALY HOUSE, 2424 Broadway, Galveston, 1889–1891

Stanford White, of McKim, Mead, and White, Architect

The home built by George Sealy in 1889 is one of the most significant nineteenth-century houses in Texas. It is also one of a very few buildings built in Texas before 1900 to have been designed by a nationally acclaimed architect. The firm of McKim, Mead, and White, of New York, was commissioned to design the house, and it is assumed to be primarily the work of Stanford White, who had by then gained a reputation for his residential designs. Although it is not one of the firm's well-known works, it is a design of merit and interest. In the materials used and in the stylistic detail it is obvious that the architect was interested in the relationship of the house to its setting and climate. In choosing a light rose-brown Belgian brick, with terra cotta for the cornice, and a red-tile roof, White achieved a definite Mediterranean character. The masses of the house are arranged in an informal composition similar to the better-known summer houses that the firm was designing at this time for its wealthy New York clients at Newport, R.I., but the architectural detail is taken from the Italian Renaissance. Thus the romantic informality of the late Victorian forms was combined with the newly revived use of Renaissance ornament. The result was a house which introduced a new style to Texas—the Renaissance Revival, a style which reached the height of its popularity in the first decade of the twentieth century.

200. THE GEORGE SEALY HOUSE (Interior Detail), 2424 Broadway, Galveston, 1889–1891

The interior of the ballroom of the Sealy House reveals the newly introduced Renaissance Revival style as handled by Stanford White.

BIBLIOGRAPHY AND INDEX

BIBLIOGRAPHY

Barnstone, Howard. *The Galveston That Was*. New York: MacMillan, 1966.

Bracken, Dorothy Kendall, and Maurine Whorton Redway. *Early Texas Homes*. Dallas: Southern Methodist University Press, 1956.

Connally, Ernest Allen. "Architecture at the End of the South: Central Texas," *Journal of the Society of Architectural Historians*, Vol. XI, No. 4 (December, 1952), pp. 8–12.

———. "Texas Architecture," *Historic Preservation*, Vol. 16, No. 6 (November–December, 1964), pp. 220–228.

Eastman, Seth. *A Seth Eastman Sketchbook, 1848–1849*. Austin: The University of Texas Press, 1961.

Evans, Elliot A. P. "The East Texas House," *Journal of the Society of Architectural Historians*, Vol. XI, No. 4 (December, 1952), pp. 1–7.

Gideon, Samuel Edward. *Historic and Picturesque Austin*. Austin: 1936.

———. "Sunday Houses in Texas," *Pencil Points* (April, 1931), pp. 277–281.

Hamlin, Talbot F. *Greek Revival Architecture in America*. New York: Oxford, 1944.

Harris, August Watkins. *Minor and Major Mansions in Early Austin*. Austin: Privately published, 1955.

———. *Minor and Major Mansions in Early Austin and Their Sequel*. Austin: Privately published, 1958.

Holley, Mary Austin. *Texas*. Austin: Steck, 1935. Facsimile of original published by J. Clarke, Lexington, Kentucky, 1836.

———. "The Texas Diary, 1835–1838," *The Texas Quarterly*, Vol. VIII, No. 2 (Summer, 1965), pp. 12–120.

Jordan, Terry G. "German Houses in Texas," *Landscape*, Vol. 14, No. 1 (Autumn, 1964), pp. 24–26.

Olmsted, Frederick Law. *Journey Through Texas*, ed. James Howard. Austin: Von Boeckmann-Jones, 1962.

Ramsdell, Charles. *San Antonio: A Historical and Pictorial Guide*. Austin: The University of Texas Press, 1959.

Roemer, Ferdinand. *Texas*, translated by Oswald Mueller. San Antonio: Standard Printing Co., 1935.

Schiwetz, E. M. *Buck Schiwetz' Texas*. Austin: The University of Texas Press, 1960.

Shuffler, R. Henderson. "Winedale Inn at Texas' Cultural Crossroad," *The Texas Quarterly*, Vol. VIII, No. 2 (Summer, 1965), pp. 129–144.

INDEX